Beachcombing
The Pacific

BEACHCOMBING
THE PACIFIC

AMOS L. WOOD

West Chester, Pennsylvania 19380

Library of Congress Cataloging in Publication Data

Wood, Amos L.
  Beachcombing the Pacific

  Bibliography: p.
  1. Beachcombing—Pacific coast (North America)
  1. Title.
  G532.6.P3W66   917.9′04′3   87-60203
  ISBN: 0-88740-097-3

Printed in the United States of America.
ISBN: 0-88740-097-3
Published by Schiffer Publishing Ltd.
1469 Morstein Road, West Chester, Pennsylvania 19380

This book may be purchased from the publisher.
Please include $2.00 postage.
Try your bookstore first.

To Elaine, Don, Ruth Mary,
and all who have left footprints
on the sands of the Pacific

Contents

Introduction

No more fascinating a place exists than a Pacific Ocean beach, for the appeal of the seashore is inborn in most of us. We may love the wheat fields of Iowa or the glaciers of Alaska, but the Pacific shores of Hawaii, California, or British Columbia will capture one's soul.

To prowl a Pacific beach is to gain release from everyday pressures. We see ourselves in a new light when we measure ourselves against a body of water that stretches beyond the horizon, all 71,000,000 square miles of it. From a San Francisco beach the Pacific stretches 4,600 miles to Soviet Russia and the port of Vladivostok. There is something satisfying in just looking at a huge body of water. The cry of the seagull, the pounding of the surf, the crashing of waves against a rocky coast are only part of the sound of the sea.

To walk a beach, kick at the surface, wonder how many grains of sand there are on the earth's surface, and consider items left along the high tide line is to qualify as a beachcomber. And with the increase in leisure time most Americans have experienced in recent years, growing numbers of people today are searching out rivers, lakes, and oceans for places to spend their newly won free time. There is nationwide interest in and attraction to ocean shores where hundreds of thousands can picnic, walk, swim, or simply relax.

Almost all of these people qualify as beachcombers, though few think of themselves as such—perhaps because, in past years, beachcombers have not enjoyed a very good image. A beachcomber was a man who lived in the South Pacific, who took up with the native women, who lived off the beach and was often a troublesome character, a tropical version of a bum. The beachcomber was a rough buccaneer rowdy who took anything off the beach he could get his hands on to trade for drink. Thus Ruby El Hult, in describing the early history of Port Townsend, Washington, on the Olympic peninsula, quoted an earlier writer as saying: "Port Townsend is a notorious resort of beachcombers and outlaws of every description."

It gets worse. A beachcomber, according to Webster, is ". . . a loafer on any of the islands of the Pacific." Roget defines him as a ". . . wanderer, vagabond, vagrant, tramp." In Mexico there is the term "Vagabando del Mar" meaning vagabond of the sea, which is also used in somewhat uncomplimentary terms.

All that may be true, I suppose, but beachcombing can be an avocation as well as a vocation, and one can get real pleasure, as well as some rewards, from an hour, an afternoon, a weekend, depending on the urge. My wife Elaine, I, and many of our friends are beachcombers, yet we are not wanderers, or tramps, or loafers. We like a good night's sleep in a comfortable bed, not on a hard sandy beach.

And we are not alone. In fact, most serious beachcombers are far more like us than they are like Webster's loafers. A more accurate definition would include any person who derives pleasure, recreation, or livelihood by searching ocean, lake, and river shores for useful or artful objects.

One may follow his own fancy as to what to look for. It need not be anything unusual. A shell will intrigue some. A small piece of wood with its grain sandblasted, a colored rock, a misshapen stone, a weathered piece of bark with its concentric pattern, a small piece of driftwood with a barnacle attached—all are items that may go into one's pocket or palm. I often pick up bits of wood to add to a collage. Elaine looks for frosted pieces of glass for her craft work. The simplest things are there for the picking. Some people beachcomb with a purpose—to expand a collection of shells, bottles, or driftwood. Others beachcomb only to discard the item as they tire of it.

One of the great pleasures of beachcombing is that there are few rules or regulations. There is no special equipment required, though, as we shall see, the serious beachcomber can benefit from much that modern science has provided, no rackets to restring, no golf balls to lose, no guns to clean. There is no special clothing required; in fact, the oldest and most decrepit clothing that you own is quite in style. No license is required; nor are there any traditions to follow. Few are the limits, tracks to follow, or courses to maintain. There is not even a score to add up afterward. If you merely get a single whiff of salt air as you approach the beach, you have already won: a carefree walk is ahead, rain or shine, night or day.

In short, anyone can beachcomb—and gain great enjoyment. Yet one can also, on the coast and on lake shores and river banks, take steps to improve the return on the effort expended. Not only are certain areas on a beach, and certain beaches, better for finding items but also certain searching techniques are more productive. A beach that collects driftwood is always better than one without. Coves are better than rocky outcroppings. High tide line gleaning is better than low tide searching. Onshore winds deposit drift at any tide, while offshore winds are poor depositors.

In short, the rewards of beachcombing are many. First are the intangibles. There is the walk. The walk may be a few steps or a few miles, whatever your fancy at the time. Whatever its duration, the salt air makes us feel new again, in tune with Mother Nature.

There is the opportunity to observe the relentless ocean and its unceasing conflict with the shoreline. No matter the arena—rocky coast, high cliffs, or wide sandy beaches—the battle goes on. Storm after storm, tide after tide, wave after wave, the struggle continues, endlessly different and fascinating.

The best reward is the serenity, the feeling of idle accomplishment, and the satisfaction that comes from this seashore search. Browsing without benefit or need of timetable relaxes one's inner self as no other elixir could.

Next there are the tangible rewards: the souvenirs to be found at the high tide line. Some are rare trophies, others almost as common as the sand itself. These latter finds—a shell, a bit of driftwood, a rock, a dried piece of kelp—we take home as reminders of the seashore, of what has taken place, and perhaps as a sign of our growth in understanding.

Aesthetics aside, some finds offer rewards in terms of trade or money. Often a lost marine item has salvage value; dimension lumber from deck cargo lost overboard has immediate trade value. Occasionally, a specific item, lost oceanographic instrumentation gear, for example, brings an established fee for the finder. Many beachcombed items that are considered oddities and consequently are unique may suddenly acquire an exaggerated price in the marketplace that has no relation to its original cost. Every beachcomber wants his collection to contain some one thing that is outstanding and a conversation piece.

With so much of value, real or aesthetic, literally lying about, waiting to be picked up, it is not surprising that the serious beachcomber is, above all, motivated.

The casual visitor to the beach takes only a short walk, has no specific purpose. The serious searcher plans his hike, selects the tide and wind conditions that are favorable, prepares for an extended trip, and has a particular objective in mind. They may be compared to the hare and the tortoise—the former flits about but the latter brings home the goodies.

When the conditions are right, the serious beachcomber is on the beach, or thinking about it. The lure of good beachcombing conditions to the ardent beachcomber may be as powerful as the inborn instinct of the salmon run upstream is to the Indian.

This book is written to capture the fun and excitement of beachcombing and also to show potential and practicing beachcombers how to go about serious beachcombing successfully.

xiii

Side of large ship on the beach at Malarrimo, Baja. (Mike McMahan Photo)

1
The Pacific Ocean—A General Survey

The geographical areas around the northern Pacific Ocean that are covered in this book are those shores that border western North America plus Hawaii and other Pacific Island groups: Baja, California, Oregon, Washington, British Columbia, Alaska, Hawaii, and other islands north of the equator.

The southern Pacific Ocean offers only mediocre beachcombing opportunities; it is the northern Pacific Ocean with its many peoples living beyond its beaches, the high incidence of activities on its stormy surface, and the well-defined ocean patterns, that is the subject of our immediate interest.

The considerable beachcombing activity that takes place on our western Pacific shores as related to other reported findings from worldwide beach locations serves as evidence of the fact that the areas bordering the northern Pacific Ocean are the most productive for beachcombing in the world. Thanks to the massive eastbound Japan Current that has a direct effect on each of our beach regions, plus other Pacific Ocean factors concerning the weather, our western Pacific Ocean shore residents reap a continuous harvest from the largest of oceans.

Baja

The first region to be included in Pacific Ocean beachcombing areas is the Baja Peninsula of western Mexico. This rough, isolated, and arid land contains over 1,600 miles of shoreline; but our focus is on the 800 miles of western beaches facing the Pacific Ocean. These outer coastal shores are uninhabited and mostly inaccessible by automobile. Some are available to the four-wheel drive rough terrain vehicle, others only by small boat.

This almost deserted peninsula now has an improved road its full length to the southern tip where the resort areas of La Paz and San Lucas are located. Except for the first 200 miles containing numerous small communities, the road is well inland most of the way and some distance from the Pacific shore. Many Pacific beaches may be as far as 100 miles from this backbone arterial highway.

One day's finds at Malarrimo Beach, Baja. (Mike McMahan Photo)

The logistics required to beachcomb portions of the Baja coast are exacting. Because desert areas border parts of the western coast, all fresh water, food, shelter, and means of locomotion have to be brought in. This is definitely not a hiking situation. Again, except for the first 200 miles to El Rosario, there are little signs of habitation and vegetation. Daytime temperatures can be in the chilling 50s with fog or a simmering 120 degrees.

The best-known beachcombing beach of Baja is at Malarrimo, which is located directly west of El Arco but is 160 miles by truck from El Arco beyond Scammons Lagoon. The difficulty in approaching this beach by land, sea, or air severely limits the visits per year. Driving on this beach may be hazardous; beach drift prevents ready approach by small landplane; and no safe anchorage exists offshore.

There are other isolated beaches of Baja that also have captured prizes from the Pacific. Timbers from early sailing vessels may favor one beach, glass fishing floats may alight on another. Boxes from World War II, airplane pieces, ocean drift bottles, oars, buoys, life jackets, and canned rations are strewn along the high tide line of this region. Erosion of the ocean sand banks by tidal waves and the creeping of coastal sand dunes by coastal winds will continue to uncover or bury Baja beachcombing trophies for years to come.

California

Almost all of the exposed ocean coast of the western continental United States is fair game for the beachcomber. However, the longest of the western coastal beach states is California with about 900 miles of shoreline. In each of its south, central, and northern coastal regions are sand beaches separated by headlands, rock outcroppings, and steep cliffs; these beaches collect driftwood, shells, and lost marine equipment.

The southern region of California from San Diego to Santa Barbara consists of a ribbon of many white sandy beaches such as those at Newport Beach, Santa Monica, and Ventura. In central California from Point Conception north another several hundred miles past San Francisco are a number of good areas like Morro Bay and Monterey Bay. In northern California from Point Reyes north past Crescent

California Pacific Ocean sand dune beach area near Morro Bay. (Harry Wenger Photo)

City is again several hundred miles of still another series of promising beaches.

Many a California beach is traversed daily by its citizenry because of the high population density next to or within a few hours' drive of the ocean, and much of California's ocean coast is readily accessible by automobile. Although parts of the oceanfront are private and barricaded, most beaches are in the public domain.

Oregon

Traveling north into Oregon, we find fewer high cliffs and rocky coasts, which provides for almost continuous sandy beaches starting from Brookings near the California border for 350 miles north to the mouth of the Columbia River. These flat sandy beaches are broken occasionally by bays, inlets, rivers, and rocky prominences. A coast highway runs the full length of Oregon, so practically all of the beaches are readily accessible by automobile; however, this wide band of sand beckons many a tourist or resident to a daily quota of salt-air recreation.

Ocean storms at this latitude drive a wide variety of beach-

Driftwood sea serpent rests on the sands at Twin Rocks, Oregon (above, left). (Burford Wilkerson Photo)   Swordgrass foothold in sand dunes at Nehalem Spit on Oregon's Pacific coast. Mount Neahkahnie is in the background (above, right).

combing trophies onto Oregon beaches—sunken ship remains, agates, driftwood, plus considerable ocean debris from the Orient. It is here that West Coast Pacific Ocean beachcombing seems to be at its very best; good beachcombing takes place at such beach areas as Gold Beach, Bandon, Coos Bay Spit, Winchester Bay, Yachats, Lincoln City, and Seaside.

This region of Oregon has a series of small coastal towns, and their residents, many of whom are retired, scour beaches day and night in their all-year-round beachcombing. It appears that in Oregon more people take long beach hikes than their counterparts do in California, perhaps due to the fact that Oregon beaches tend to be longer.

Washington

North of the Columbia River entrance begin 150 miles of Washington State's Pacific Ocean coast. For the first 75 miles, there are wide, flat sandy beaches extending ahead, broken only by the occasional bay, inlet, or river. These beaches are well known for their exceptional beachcomber findings, especially for the oriental debris deposited there from numerous coastal storms. Winter weather patterns here not only bring southwesterly storms of gale proportions, but also bring in the debris carried offshore by the Japan Current. The beachcombing at places like Long Beach, Grayland, Ocean Shores, Copalis, and Pacific Beach is excellent.

About mid-state, north of Moclips, is the Quinault Indian Reservation, which extends for about 25 miles, but this is not accessible to the public. Further on begins the 50-mile Pacific Ocean strip of the Olympic National Park, which extends from Kalaloch north past the Ozette Indian Reservation. For most of this northern half of the coast there are rocky shores with shingle and steep gravel areas; however, certain beach locations such as those at Kalaloch, La Push, and Ozette are regularly sought out by the serious beachcomber, even though it may mean a long hike. At the extreme northern tip of the state, the Makah Indian Reservation again limits access by the public.

A rock-bound shore typical of Washington's northern Pacific coastline. (Weldon W. Rau Photo)

Because of deep inlets, bays, and unfavorable coastal terrain, Washington does not have a full-length coast highway such as Oregon is blessed with. The existing coast highway makes the Washington coast accessible by automobile only at four points, and even then only for relatively short distances. There are few places where one can even see the Pacific Ocean from this highway.

Some of the beaches are hiked into from one end and out the other. Since no motor vehicles are allowed in the Olympic National Park strip, numerous backpack hikers are seen year-round hiking beaches such as those between La Push and Ozette, a distance of about 20 miles. This entails a hike of two to three days duration depending on tides and progress across the headlands. There are occasional shelters to bunk in and wildlife such as bears to watch for, but there is beachcombing to be had all along the way—all that can be carried out in your pack.

There are few large-sized communities along these ocean beaches, so the population density is low enough to make every beachcombing hike or even an afternoon's walk a success.

Steep cliffs and cobble beach of Pacific coast south of Queets, Washington, is part of Quinault Indian Reservation. (Weldon W. Rau Photo)

British Columbia

Canada's sole claim to the Pacific Ocean is through the Province of British Columbia. Its shoreline consists of over 500 miles of continuous rugged inlets. The Coast Mountains cascade close to shore, so good beaches for beachcombing in British Columbia are few and far between. What they lack in number they do make up in quality. They are generally isolated but available to the fisherman, hunter, and prospector.

Vancouver Island, which blankets the southern one-third of the British Columbia coast from direct Pacific Ocean action, has on its own outer coast a number of outstanding beaches. Most of these are

Beach drift logs spread along in a partially protected cove on isolated Bartlett Island off the British Columbia Pacific coast (top).

Typical isolated beach scene on Bartlett Island off the west coast of Vancouver Island. Last high tide line is above even with beach rocks at right hand side of the photo (above).

accessible only by boat or by air. One exception is the 12-mile-long Wickaninnish Bay strip named Long Beach about halfway between Ucluelet and Tofino. This beach is now accessible by the recently surfaced winding road through the mountains from Port Alberni. This beach, now within the boundary of the Pacific Rim National Park, is considered the finest recreation beach in all of Canada. In 1960, following a week of exceptional beachcombing for Japanese glass fishing floats, I considered it one of the world's finest beaches for beachcombing. Now with the road open and the numerous park campsites alongside this beautiful flat beach, the beachcombing is better further north on the island.

The Queen Charlotte Island group, offshore from the northern British Columbia coast, is about 180 miles in length with many deep inlets and rocky shores. The occasional sandy beach here produces excellent beachcombing for the hearty. The northeastern and eastern shores of Graham Island are prime areas accessible by road from Skidegate to Tlell and Masset. The rest of the Queen Charlottes are accessible only by boat or by air. The outer western side of this island group is exceedingly rugged, isolated, and treacherous—certainly no place for the uninitiated.

The British Columbia coast between Vancouver Island and the Queen Charlottes is wild and inaccessible except for the road to Bella Coola from the inland city of Williams Lake 300 miles to the east. There is beachcombing to be had in this region, but the logistics of getting into this part of British Columbia are not simple.

Most British Columbia beaches are isolated and will remain that way for some time to come. There is no British Columbia coastal highway nor is there promise of one—ever. Hopefully, like the trout fishing in the Province of British Columbia, its beachcombing will remain good for the near future—at least until this part of Canada is "discovered" by its easterners.

Alaska

To beachcomb in Alaska means flying to numerous places like Ketchikan, Wrangell, Sitka, Hoonah, Juneau, Cordova, the Kenai Peninsula, Kodiak, Bristol Bay, Coal Harbor, Adak, Kiska, Attu, and the Pribilof Islands. Alaska has the longest shoreline of any western

Pacific state, but only a small fraction of this is available for beach-combing. Almost the entire shoreline is rocky. Since few, if any, of the 4,000 miles of coast are accessible by automobile, the beaches that do collect Pacific Ocean debris will hold what is collected for long periods.

Once you have arrived on an Alaskan beach there are usually good pickings. The more remote and the harder it is to approach, the better is the beachcombing. In Alaska there are a wide variety of both man-made and nature-made objects that can be found. Alaska is so big and so unpopulated that its beachcombing, like most everything else, is tremendous and relatively noncompetitive. Unfortunately, for every glass fishing float that is beached in the sand, there must be a dozen that get bashed to bits on the rocks; for every ship timber that comes in, there are another dozen that get buried in the sand.

Practically all visits to Alaskan beaches are by boat or by airplane. Pilots will land on a beach where the gravel or sand is packed hard enough to support a small airplane; however, in certain seasons the sands may be too soft for a safe landing. I have listened to accounts told by pilot friends of flying a small two-place land plane into a short curved beach with a sloping gravel shore edge, and land-ing in order to pick up large glass fishing floats that they had spotted while flying by. Other beachcombing pilots will bring small float planes onto rivers or lakes that are adjacent to or near outer exposed saltwater beaches. One pilot friend ties his small float plane to the kelp alongside a rocky outcropping, then rows ashore in an inflatable raft through the ocean's surf to the beach. On these beach visits the limit of what can be brought back is the volume and weight limita-tion remaining in the small airplane after the pilot and his passenger have squeezed in for the return flight.

Where there is a protected anchorage for fishermen to bring their boats into, any nearby beaches will be combed, particularly when bad weather will drive them in to shelter. Many an unusual item has been picked up by a fisherman who has rowed ashore with his dog in the dinghy in order to stretch his legs on solid ground after running in ahead of bad weather to a safe anchorage. This often well-earned diversion will bring him an unexpected dividend.

It is generally not easy for a tourist to get passage to some beach

This sunset beach scene at Nelson Lagoon, Alaska, shows one of the few remaining fishing stake nets. Gill net is strung on poles set out offshore and salmon are "beachcombed" from small boats when the tide is high (above, left). (Doris Cowden Photo)   A petrified cedar stump is examined during extremely low tide near Sand Point, Alaska (above, right). (Lyle A. Hansen Photo)

with a fisherman for two reasons. First, the fisherman is probably heading somewhere that precludes picking anyone up again; and second, his insurance may not cover a passenger. At some places, a water taxi may be available for charter, but be prepared to pay handsomely for this service. Although local people can take you to beaches known to have good beachcombing, Alaskan beaches are seldom worked by outsiders. It is the fisherman, hunter, and prospector who get to the isolated beaches. The favored corporation prospectors get to visit prime isolated sites thanks to their field work helicopter charter services.

For visits to a distant beach, the tourist can charter a pilot to drop him off and pick him up on a return trip a few days later. The logistics of this type of beachcombing expedition are simple enough. Bring along enough gear to take care of the degree of creature comforts desired—for example, tent, sleeping bag, food, water, cooking stove, and rifle for protection. The sad part is that there will not be enough room or weight allowance in the small airplane on the return trip to carry all the beachcombed items you want to bring home. Then there will be the spot decisions alongside the airplane before takeoff—what to bring out, what to discard—and the discards will haunt you for the rest of your days.

Hawaii

Our fiftieth state, the Hawaiian Island group, is strategically located at the crossroads of the Pacific Ocean. These islands are situated within the circulatory pattern of the major Pacific Ocean currents and happen to border the strong westbound North Equatorial Current. Much of the existing plant life on these islands arrived on these same ocean currents following the volcanic formation of this mid-ocean outpost.

Lauhala-fringed Lumahai Beach is one of Kauai's most beautiful scenic attractions. (Hawaii Visitors Bureau Photo)

Hawaiian Island beachcombing is affected by Pacific Ocean currents and by meteorological factors. Here steady northeast trade winds blow throughout the year to bring in a modest amount of fishing gear and bottles, among many other collectibles. Usually near the end of the year there is a two-week period of storms and torrential rains that are accompanied by strong southeast winds, so-called Kona (bad) winds, named because they come from the direction of the Kona beach on the large island of Hawaii. These storms drive in ocean drift from the nearby North Equatorial Current, thus making some of the southern beach areas good locations to beachcomb during this period.

Each of the main islands has unique geographical features, but all have some beaches even if they are only short stretches or small pockets separated by rock outcroppings. Lush vegetation grows on the windward coasts of the islands because of the heavy rainfall created by the moisture-laden trade winds. The leeward sides of the islands are dry and barren. Steady trade winds also carry large glass fishing floats to the islands. Many of these balls are seen displayed in yards and in homes.

Three favorite beaches for the beachcomber to try that collect ocean drift are: Kaalualu on the south shore of Hawaii, Kapaa on Kauai, and Kailua on Oahu. These are all accessible by automobile.

Much of the beach sand of the Hawaiian Islands is pure white; however, at some areas the sand may be of a light brown color. The beaches here are well combed principally because of the many shells of all sizes that are found.

Rivers and Lakes

Many rivers and lakes that feed into the Pacific also have sandy beaches and shallow waters to search. Although freshwater beachcombing may not have the variety of things that are found on ocean beaches, the monetary return can be greater. For example: prospecting for gold in streams and beachcombing for semiprecious stones along river banks are popular weekend activities. Many a discarded item thrown into a river at high water is readily detected during low water—and if you are lucky, the discarded item may have historical value. Historical artifacts can be hunted along streams at sites where explorers and fur traders might have made camp. Tools, fishing implements, and weapons lost by Indians as they moved about are another type of artifact sought by river combers. For a taste of river beachcombing, try the Sacramento in California, the Umpqua in Oregon, the Columbia in Washington, or the Thompson in British Columbia.

Lakes are categorized by elevation, and it is this factor that will make a great difference in your beachcombing success. Lowland lakes are above tidal levels sometimes by only a few feet, while upland lakes are usually at foothill or mountain elevations where the lake level will change seasonally. Both usually contain walkable beaches, and most West Coast lakes are accessible. Where upland lake levels change seasonally, there will be surprises along the exposed shores for the observant lake shore beach hiker.

For transportation around small lakes, a dinghy with a small

Beachcombing on the shores of Lake Washington. Note the three different drift lines made by the previous evening's waves.

outboard is best. A faster boat and its deeper draft will not have the mobility required for shore contact. Maneuverability is most important in and around tree branches and logs that often border on uninhabited shores. At upland lakes there is often a brisk afternoon wind that will set in without warning, so don't get caught in your dinghy without enough gas or oarpower to beat your way back to the starting point. For lowland lakes, learn of the prevailing winds before starting out.

Some favorite beachcombing areas are Clear Lake in California, Upper Klamath Lake in Oregon, Lake Washington in Washington, and Lake Okanagan in British Columbia.

The Japan Current

Current and storm patterns of the northern Pacific Ocean determine the beachcombing to be had along our western coastal shores. These current patterns are massive and the weather patterns are complex, but understandably so since this ocean covers almost half of the surface of the globe. Although Pacific Ocean current patterns are generally understood, the weather patterns are not. A relationship is believed to exist between this ocean and its accompanying weather, but this has yet to have professional concurrence.

Charts made every month of ocean current direction and speed for navigation purposes show the principal current pattern of the northern Pacific to resemble a flattened out figure eight, the lower lobe having a clockwise direction and the upper lobe having a counterclockwise flow. These charts also show that the important current is the central eastbound current, centered at about the 45th parallel. The Japanese call this current *Kuroshio*, meaning "black stream," so called because of its darker color.

Other parts of the northern Pacific circulatory pattern have been given names that describe their geographical location, such as the California Current that heads south along the California coast. The North Equatorial Current is the fast westbound current at about the 11th parallel, or along the bottom of the figure eight, which stretches from Baja to the Philippines to become one of the longest currents of the world. At the top of the upper loop is another westbound current named the Alaska Current, which heads past the Aleutian chain toward Russia.

Still the biggest, most powerful, and dominant current of all is the Kuroshio or Japan Current. This current is singularly responsible for the array of oriental items that are found on our western shores. Even whole fishing junks, perhaps a hundred all told, have covered the distance to America as derelicts. Thousands of oriental manufactured glass fishing floats carried by Kuroshio are beached each year along North American shores, while millions more plus other oriental oddities are riding the big figure eight waiting for a coastal storm to drive them ashore. Approaching our shores it is known as the North Pacific Current.

Beachcombed whiskey bottle has well-developed hairdo of gooseneck barnacles acquired while drifting upside down in Pacific Ocean coastal currents. (Bert Webber Photo)

2

A Catalogue of Pacific Treasures

The Pacific thrusts upon its shores a wide variety of man-made goods and nature-grown harvests. The waves, winds, and currents of the largest of oceans carry buoyant items thousands of miles, and things not so buoyant are rolled long distances along the bottom of the sea— finally to come to rest on a beach somewhere. Any beachcomber fortunate enough to live near an ocean beach can attest to the wide spectrum of items that can be discovered and carried home.

MAN-MADE OBJECTS

Man-made items can be classified into general groupings such as glass, wood, plastic, and metal. What I describe below are just some of the more common things—it would be impossible to list everything you can find—you can expect to come upon on any one of a hundred Pacific beaches.

Glassware

Bottles

Bottle collecting is now a very popular nationwide pastime. Bottle collectors haunt old houses, dumps and fills, mining and logging camps; skin diving collectors search in harbors and around piers.

Equally as many bottles are found by beachcombers on Pacific Ocean beaches, and bottle beachcombers also are likely to come across bottles of almost any national origin.

Bottle thrown into the Pacific took two years to travel to the Oregon coast. (Burford Wilkerson Photo)

Beachcombers often find bottles containing messages written by children while vacationing at a beach. These bottles are washed up in proximity to where they were dropped into a stream or from a dock or a boat. The content reflects the thoughts of the youthful sender. An example of this is the one I found on our beach on Lake Washington, near Seattle. It was written in pencil and came in a glass peanut butter jar. It read, "I am Sandra Hill. I live in Bellevue, Washington. I have a cat. I am eight years old."

Another type of bottle message comes from young adults looking for pen pals. Although these messages may be amusing, the bottles rarely have any value for the finder—unless, of course, the message sparks a friendship with the sender. (I know of one case in which the messages sent by two individuals actually led to marriage.)

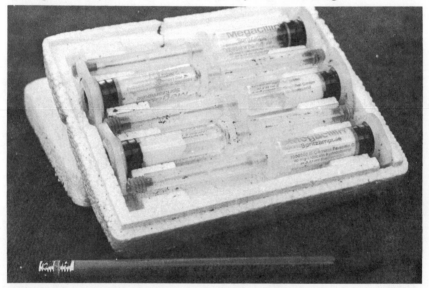

A penicillin medical kit, presumably lost from a fishing boat, was beachcombed on the Olympic National Park coast near Lake Ozette, Washington.

Pill Bottles

Beachcombers get to know the medical problems of Japanese fishermen hundreds of miles away by examining pill bottles that are found strewn in the driftwood, although most of the bottles are empty.

One bottle with a prescription was found on an isolated Vancouver Island beach; it was dated only two weeks before by a Tokyo drugstore. Also of medical interest, one occasionally finds plastic syringes.

Drift Bottles

A great deal of experimentation has taken place with drift bottles and drift plastic envelopes used by oceanography organizations to examine ocean currents. Most drift bottles contain a card printed in several languages—usually English, Japanese, and Russian, and sometimes Spanish. A reward of one dollar is often offered to the finder, who is asked to write on the card the place of finding and the date. With this information, the approximate speed and direction of the current is established. A great number of these bottles and envelopes have been dropped at different places in the Pacific by such organizations as:

United States Department of Commerce, Coast and Geodetic
    Survey
Oregon State University, Department of Oceanography
Fisheries Research Board, Canada
Tokyo University of Fisheries
Formosa Free China Fisheries Company
Russia Vladivostok University
University of Washington

Drift bottle with note took 965 days to travel from Japan to Rockaway, Oregon (left). (Burford Wilkerson Photo)   Message block used by United States Coast Guard to drop messages from Coast Guard airplanes to disabled vessels or beach rescue groups (above).

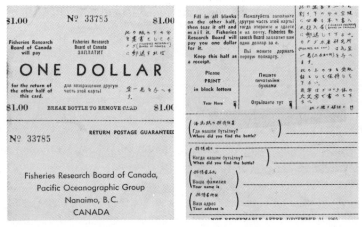

One of the return cards from a beachcombed drift bottle used in an ocean current experiment. Cards are rolled up and slid through the necks of bottles to open up as shown.

Research drift bottles are clear in appearance so that the card inside is readily visible. In a typical drift bottle experiment, about four percent of the total number of bottles released will be discovered and reported.

Position Bottles

Another group of bottle messages is the now-outmoded "position bottles" thrown overboard from merchant ships and containing navigational information; the messages indicated that on noon of a certain day the ship was at a specific latitude and longitude. With the advent of radio navigation, this practice has been discontinued.

Passengers, however, may toss bottles with messages overboard, and occasionally these are picked up on some distant shore.

Light Bulbs

Pacific Ocean beaches are strewn with light bulbs. From time to time large light bulbs have beached, some of them as much as two feet long and looking like huge radio tubes—these light bulbs are lighthouse bulbs.

Large, five-hundred watt, blue glass light bulbs also are found— these are Japanese, Chinese, and Korean long line tuna boat night-fishing light bulbs.

Smaller, household-sized, oriental light bulbs are beachcombed regularly in the Pacific Northwest, although they are not highly valued. In fact, sometimes beachcombers bury these bulbs in the sand

Silhouette of a beachcombed lighthouse light bulb. This lamp, when encased in a lighthouse lens housing, projects a beam at night that can be seen twenty miles at sea.

with just enough of the glass showing to simulate the appearance of Japanese glass fishing floats—to fool the next person that comes that way.

Burned out radio vacuum tubes are also occasionally found.

Saki Jugs

Perhaps the most colorful of all the bottles beachcombed are large Japanese saki jugs. The equivalent of our carboy or demijohn, they have a distinctive and characteristic blue color, hold about four gallons, and weigh nearly twelve pounds. Some have a large letter K imprinted on the bottom. They are much sought after by interior decorators and bring a good price, though few of those that are beachcombed trade hands.

Beachcomber Doris Cowden displays a two-liter, light blue Japanese saki bottle found near Nelson Lagoon, Alaska (above, left).   This saki bottle, photographed just as it was found on Vancouver Island, is considered a rare find and is highly prized because of the Japanese markings on the bottom edge (above, center).   Unusual ribbed saki bottle beachcombed on the Queen Charlotte Islands, British Columbia (above, right).

Ginger Jars

About 1960 a number of octagonal porcelain ginger jars about seven inches high were found along the Oregon and Washington coast. The jars were still sealed and contained ginger sticks. They appeared to be part of some cargo lost at sea and quickly disappeared from the beaches—to appear later on the shelves of their beachcombing finders. Once I saw several in a locked storefront, but that is the closest I have come to one. These ginger jars showed up on the beach in the region of Cannon Beach, Oregon, and Grayland, Washington, but only the favored few early morning, high tide hikers got in on the find.

Miscellaneous Glassware

Numbers of glass jars with lids screwed in place, lost overboard from trawler fishing boats, have survived the pounding surf. Perhaps a partially filled jar of peanut butter, raspberry jam, or lard will be found intact in the high tide drift line. Ketchup bottles seem particularly well designed to withstand the rough ride through the surf.

Glass insulators from telegraph poles make their way into beach drift—sometimes poles, wooden cross ties, and all. Collectors also look for glass insulators at inland areas where there is lots of sunshine to tint the glass.

I know of several ship's porthole fixtures with the glass intact found in beach sands where ship remains were buried. These are much sought after for use in beach cabins.

In about 1969 a number of twelve-inch mercury thermometers showed up along the Oregon coast. They appeared to be of a type used in scientific experimentation and worth perhaps ten dollars

Beachcomber Evelyn Morse shows size of blue glass jug she found at Nelson Lagoon, Alaska.

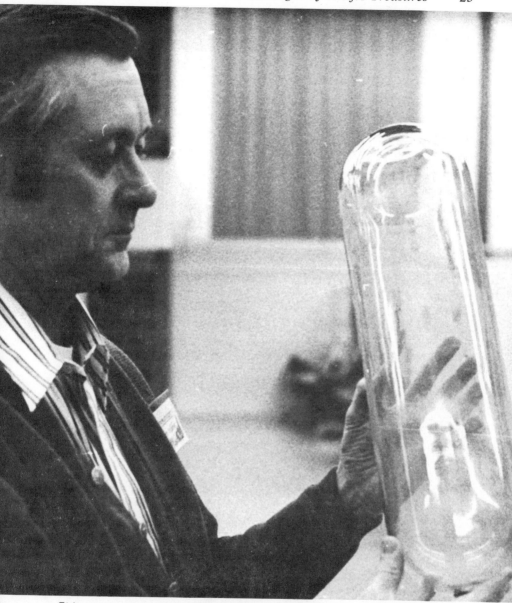

This unusual lavender-tinted sealed glass cylinder was beachcombed on the Oregon coast. Its high quality of manufacture would indicate possible use as early as 1915 for scientific purposes.

apiece. I found a small ampule on Vancouver Island still containing its unknown drug.

Beach glass, small pieces of broken glass frosted from sand abrasion, is beachcombed for use in collages. Of many colors and hues, these irregular-shaped pieces are from glass fishing floats, bottles, or jars that get broken after they have been deposited on the beach by an extremely high tide. During a heavy surf, the pulverizing action of the waves may break up a glass container and immediately bury the pieces in the sand. Occasionally a glass float will roll from the crest of a large wave onto a flat sandy beach and suddenly disappear, leaving no trace of its broken pieces. On a gravel or cobble beach, a bottle or float will usually break up during the beaching; however, its pieces will remain and be readily recognizable. After a few tides have rolled back and forth across the gravel, the edges of the glass pieces will get well rounded off, and frosted besides—ideal for one's beach glass collection.

Fishing Gear and Floats

Fishing gear of all types and the floats used to buoy this gear are picked up by the beachcomber for display or possible future use. Hooks, nets, line, lures, buoys, crab pots, and wicker baskets are usually colorful enough to attract even the uninitiated newcomer.

Two of the numerous mystery baskets that washed ashore at Tillamook, Oregon. (Burford Wilkerson Photo)

Buoy Floats

Net buoy floats are fashioned from cedar, cork, glass, and plastic, though economic pressures have caused the replacement of cork and cedar with glass and plastic, depending on the degree of mechanization in the fishery operation. Blown glass floats are still the mainstay of the oriental long line tuna fishery with its hand labor

Japanese glass fishing floats of this unique roller shape are rare and much sought after by beachcombers. Although they are believed to have been used in oriental narcotics traffic during the early 1930s, no definite information on their manufacture or use has yet been uncovered (above, left). Glass floats, Russian metal floats, and other gear found on Netarts Spit, Oregon, after a coastal storm (above, right). (Burford Wilkerson Photo)

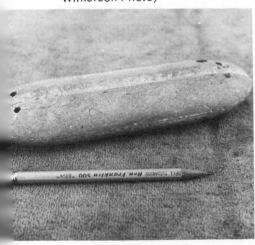

This plastic float of oriental manufacture is typical of those found along Pacific Ocean beaches. It is used by mid-Pacific fishing operations to buoy gill nets of undersized mesh (above, left). The world's largest float ever beachcombed displayed at the Seaside, Oregon, Beachcomber's Festival (above, right).

New type plastic floats used in Russian trawler fishing operations (above, left).   An array of glass floats beachcombed near Port Heiden, Alaska: (foreground) orange-sized gill net glass floats used extensively in the Bristol Bay salmon fisheries; (background) king crab tangle net marker floats—those with closely woven manila hemp rope coverings are of Japanese manufacture, those with open woven colored cotton rope are typical of Russian manufacture (above, right). (Dick Hamlin Photo)

operation, while plastic floats are standard with the American salmon gill net fishery that employs hydraulic-driven winch blocks to do the net hauling. The handblown glass float has not been replaced by plastic in other kinds of oriental fishery, popular opinion to the contrary, for the glass float is still the least expensive.

Tuna Line Lights

Located across the vast Pacific Ocean are Japanese long line tuna fishing operations. Each tuna boat strings out a single line perhaps thirty to fifty miles long, supported by numerous glass floats the size of basketballs that are attached every few hundred feet. At almost every mile, a glass float is attached with a wire frame lashed to it containing a light stanchion on the top and a battery in a case on the bottom. The purpose of the light is to show at night where a break in the line has occurred, should that happen. These floats and their

This Japanese-made barnacle-laden marker buoy was beachcombed at Ocean Shores, Washington. Batteries within the upper cylindrical portion power the light at the top.

frames occasionally make it to North America's western shores. I know of perhaps a half dozen that have been found between Alaska and Baja, Mexico. When cleaned up and painted, they make fine conversation pieces for the family room, particularly if the batteries are still good and the lights work.

Bamboo Poles

Occasionally a bamboo pole comes ashore. Usually it is about ten feet long, two inches in diameter and in good condition. One I saw had a series of cork floats tied in place toward one end. Another had a large glass marker float lashed about midway, with a rock at one end and a small flag at the other. These are used as marker poles in long line tuna fishery on the open sea and also as position markers in the king crab tangle net fishing in Alaska. Sometimes a small wooden tag is attached at the upper end, for location identification.

Nets

Beachcombers occasionally find complete fishing nets on Pacific beaches, and they are prized as attractive backdrops for wall displays. The nets can be found on the shores of Alaska, Canada, and the western United States. Few of the older, cord nets are found now; those made with synthetic fibers are the most common. Many commercial

This live seal pup entangled in a piece of fishing net was beached at Long Beach, Washington. (Chinook Observer Photo)

nets that are caught and lost on some underwater projection are so well hung up that they stay put. The smaller nets used by Indians at river entrances are more apt to be found. However, finding the net is only the beginning. The nylon net I once discovered was so completely entwined in the driftwood that considerable effort was required to dislodge it. Even after I got it home, it took hours to get it straightened out and to remove all the twigs and other foreign material.

Lines

Many short pieces of commercial nylon fishing line collect along Pacific Northwest shores. These castoff nylon ends float ashore and are still usable; while the manila line used formerly would sink to the bottom, and when it is found on the beach it is likely to be rotten. Nylon line comes in a variety of widths and colors. To illustrate, last summer I picked up samples of eighteen different types of nylon line from one-eighth inch to one inch in diameter, on the half-mile wide beach of Cox Bay, Vancouver Island, British Columbia. The colors included white, pink, yellow, red, green, blue, and black, with two of these colors on some.

Gear Trays

Round flat trays about two feet in diameter, woven of bamboo strips and rattan, are beachcombed on rare occasions. These trays are believed to be the oriental poor man's fishing kit. When not in use, the several fishing lines attached to the rim are laid around inside the tray; later, the tray is used to carry home the fish that are caught. Since these trays are thought to be used in small boats in rivers of the

Oriental fisherman's tray found on the Queen Charlotte Islands.

Orient, not many are lost—and fewer still hold up for the long ocean trip to American shores. The tray I have was found in the Queen Charlotte Islands off the coast of Canada.

Markers

Another choice find, and quite a rare item besides, is a Japanese fishing company marker flag. The only one I know about was found in the Pribilof Islands, off Nome, Alaska, in the Bering Sea. It is a red

Japanese fishing company flag found in Alaska.

rectangular flag, twenty inches by thirty inches, with black Japanese markings giving the symbol of the fishing company, the name of the ship, and the name of the mother ship.

Crab Pots

Pacific Northwest beachcombers who find commercial crab pots caught in the surf and are able to retrieve them usually receive a double benefit. The first reward is the crabs inside. The males larger than six inches across the shell in front of the points are legal and can be kept, the rest must be thrown back to protect future harvests. If the crab pot still has the nylon line and float marker attached, the owner is then readily located. When the pot is returned, the owner will usually reward you with a sizable number of live crabs already caught in other pots, or if it is a large operation they will offer a monetary reward, perhaps up to one-half the cost of a new pot.

This beachcombed crab pot became so entangled in sea growth that it had to be plucked clean before further use.

Crab Pot Floats

Crab pot marker floats and line sometimes will break away, leaving the crab pot to its watery grave. These marker buoys are as individual as their owners. Some markings consist of a unique arrangement of painted stripes on a piece of cedar wood. Another crabber

Examples of beachcombed crab pot marker buoys used by Pacific Northwest commercial crabbers.

used a series of plastic collars of different colors. Out in the ocean it is important that the crab pot buoys of each crabber are easily recognized, consequently there are numerous colorful and individual markings.

Steel Floats

In recent years, Russian fishing operations have moved into Alaskan and American West Coast waters with fleets of trawlers, mother ships, and canneries. A friend once counted fifty of these ships as they lined the horizon off the Oregon coast. Beachcombers soon know of their presence from the numerous steel fishing floats lost from these trawlers. The floats are manufactured from two hemispherical

Russian-manufactured metal float beachcombed off the outer coast of Vancouver Island.

Rugged aluminum fishing floats attached to heavy duty fishing net provide an artistic foregound at a small boat harbor at Crescent City, California. (Bert Webber Photo)

halves welded together, but they contain no protective coating. Because of their rusty and uninviting appearance, these floats hold little appeal to the beachcomber. They come in several sizes, roughly six, twelve, eighteen, and twenty-four inches in diameter. The larger ones contain a hollow steel tube inside to enable threading onto a cable. These are quite heavy and are rarely moved far from their beached location. Most float collectors will add one of these floats to their collection just to acknowledge their existence.

Inflatable Floats

Occasionally an inflatable float will be found. There is a type that is used in long line tuna fishing operations that is roughly basketball size. Another variety is about two feet in diameter and orange in color and is used in Alaskan king crab fishing.

Wooden Objects

All kinds of pieces of timber are found along Pacific Ocean shores, many of which come from trees indigenous to the Orient:

cedar, spruce, fir, alder, mahogany, sandalwood, teak, gum, redwood, myrtlewood, oak, maple, birch, hemlock, yew, sen, cypress, and others. Beachcombers often collect standard-sized samples of these woods for identification and display.

Dimension Lumber

Beachcombed planks of dimension lumber are readily used in the construction of small homes, garages, work sheds, and other similar shelters.

Occasionally ship deck loads of dimension lumber (usually fir, hemlock, or spruce) will wash overboard, and thanks to the ocean currents and maelstroms that tend to keep such flotsam together, it will often beach in a specific locality. Many a time large amounts of fresh clean lumber, without a sign of a barnacle, will arrive unannounced at a particular beach and yet not be identified with any shipwreck or storm at sea. On such occasions beachcombers bring their automobiles or trucks to the beach to haul loads away. With the present price of lumber, it is worthwhile to carry home even a short piece of dimension lumber.

Japanese equivalent of an American four-by-four comes to rest on the beach at Cape Lookout, Oregon. (Burford Wilkerson Photo)

A great deal of special-sized, oriental wood dunnage arrives on beaches all the way from Alaska to Baja. Dunnage is the loose material used to protect cargo and to provide space between cargoes for tie down, stowage, and removal.

Short length of cedar lumber beachcombed on the Washington coast. The Japanese markings roughly translate as "commercial grade, square, finished cedar" (above, left).   These samples of oriental woods beachcombed on West Coast shores are traded among wood collectors. Identification and origin is given at the left end; U.S. Forest Laboratory identification number is in the center; and location of find, finder's initials and date are given at the right end (above, right).

Japanese dunnage is found on almost any beach of the Pacific Northwest. The length of these pieces varies from two to sixteen feet; the lumber is square, three inches on a side. Because it is slabbed from small trees, many pieces taper out so that only two surfaces are flat. Often the dunnage will have Japanese characters stenciled or painted along one side indicating packing information and name of shipper. Pieces so marked containing some of the bark on the unsawed surfaces provide colorful accents for family or recreation room, especially when preserved with a clear lacquer finish.

Nameplates and Signs

Why signs and nameplates end up in the ocean to float for long distances is beyond me, yet they do. A Los Angeles, California, flood control district limit sign was found on Baja shores. A house nameplate appeared on an isolated shore of Vancouver Island. Probably some signs fall into the sea when part of a bank slides away, but if every sign I have found represents a bluff that has caved away, the

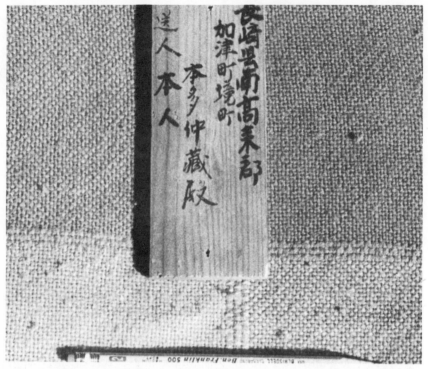

The Japanese markings on this wooden nameplate translate: "Mr. Nakazo Motoda, Kagami-cho Kasecho, Minami-Korakugan, Nagasaki-ken."

whole Pacific coast is in trouble. Vandalism may account for some signs, and general disposal of trash for others.

Ship Flotsam

Throughout the years, ships of many nations have been lost at sea. The remains of some have been identified; others still remain a mystery. Floating wreckage of a ship or its cargo may be found on any Pacific beach.

Crates

Colorful and well-marked fruit crates show up occasionally on our beaches. They contain markings in English, Chinese, Japanese, French, Norwegian, Portuguese, Swedish, and other languages. Many of these crates are found in very good condition and come from cargo ships, tramp steamers, and oil tankers that take on provisions in foreign ports. With the considerable ship traffic into the Los Angeles area, San Francisco Bay, Columbia River, and Straits of Juan de Fuca, beachcombers from Alaska to Baja reap a good harvest.

Shipwreck Materials

For years derelict oriental sampans and junks have been deposited by the Japanese Kuroshio Current around the North Pacific Rim, particularly on western American shores. Over seventy-five wrecks have been recorded, and the actual number of wrecks may be double that figure. Survivors of these wrecks and their progeny are mentioned in early Pacific Northwest history.

Recently some of the food containers, called mystery jugs, believed to have been carried on board these junks have been beachcombed.

Some of the remains of the Norwegian vessel Struan, *which was beached in 1890, uncovered by a coastal storm near Nectucca Bay, Oregon. (Burford Wilkerson Photo)*

Boat wreckage found among the driftwood at Cox Bay, British Columbia.

In 1965 near Ocean Shores, Washington, the Catala *foundered during a wind storm. The second photograph, taken in 1968, clearly shows the ravages of the sea and the souvenir hunters. (Dick Benham Photos)*

Fastenings

Most wooden ship wreckage—knee, bulkhead, plank, decking, and spars—has been salvaged long ago, of course; wooden head boards of early sailing ships, with the ship's name and port chiseled in, are valued marine trophies. But occasionally a sunken wreck still will send a wooden piece ashore. For example, one find on the shores of the Pribilof Islands in Alaska was a sailing ship dead-eye made from lignum vitae, a wood heavier than water. In addition, one can still find hand-forged, wrought-iron fittings or castings of copper and brass on occasion—both from wooden sailing ships. Because of their weight and historical interest they are often displayed at maritime museums. Rudder fittings, mast fittings, hinges, and brackets all fall into this class. The single most valuable item is the ship's bell of cast bronze, which usually is engraved with the ship's name, port of registry, and launching year.

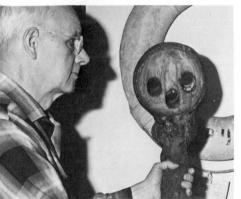 

This object, believed to be a futtock shroud fitting from the shipwreck of an old sailing vessel, was beachcombed on the Oregon coast (above, left). (Burford Wilkerson Photo)   Alaska beachcomber displays a strange, flat wooden box believed to be a talisman that was found near Nelson Lagoon, Alaska (above, right).

The hulls, superstructure, and masts of wrecked steel vessels seldom move, but some of the equipment breaks loose and beaches. Usually these pieces are small, comparatively light—for example, one friend found a ship's compass buried in a sand bank. But the pieces are not always small. The steam boiler of the *J. Harhoffer* washed up in 1910, for example, giving the name to Boiler Bay, Oregon. The boiler is still there.

A weather-beaten ship's hatch cover found on Vancouver Island. With restoration, it may end up as a rustic coffee table.

Hatch Covers

The Pacific Northwest receives its full share of hatch covers, which are heavy, usually about thirty inches wide, seventy inches long, and three inches thick—and not easily moved from their usual resting place, high in the driftwood. A coating of plastic preserves the wood grain and metal edges. Although many end up as table tops in restaurants and bars, hatch covers also provide an appropriate backdrop for displays with a nautical theme.

Furniture and Fittings

Pieces of furniture keep showing up on many beaches. For example, parts of chairs, dresser drawers, shelving, tables, and other assorted objects were beachcombed along Washington beaches following the flooding of the Columbia River. However, floods of the rivers on the West Coast are rare, and most such pieces come from the wrecks of fishing vessels; a major wreck off Vancouver Island in 1942 deposited a desk, chairs, and baby grand piano on an outer beach.

Life Rings

Beachcombed life rings enliven any marine display because of their identification with hardship and disaster. In my opinion, the choicest ones are those with neatly painted Japanese characters giving the ship's name and port of registry. Life rings lost from Russian ships are usually extremely crudely lettered by comparison. However, life rings from American, British, German, Dutch, Swedish, and Norwegian vessels are beautifully lettered in ship-shape fashion.

Life ring lost overboard from a Japanese fishing vessel was beachcombed near Port Heiden, Alaska. (Dick Hamlin Photo)

Oceanographic Gear

Not uncommonly, oceanographic research and scientific gear is found, as are marker buoys and sailboat race markers. Occasionally an organization needing a lost item, such as an instrumented buoy, will offer a reward for its return. Such an announcement will motivate beachcombers, and a lot of beach miles will be covered. It isn't very often that beachcombed items can be converted into cash directly, so there is high incentive in the search.

Edibles

It is a rare beachcombing hike I take without finding food along the tide lines. California oranges, Bermuda onions, Washington apples, lemons, coconuts, cranberries, green peppers, jars of jam, peanut butter, and lard are the most prevalent. The perishables never make it to shore. Perhaps it is only those items that have thick skins that survive the surf.

Many a flapjack has been made along the Washington coast from a beachcombed one-hundred-pound sack of flour from cargo that was lost during a Pacific storm. After submersion, the flour hardens on the outside, forming a shell about one inch thick, but the flour inside the shell remains unspoiled. Such a hardened sack is hauled home and stood upright to dry out. Then a small portion of the shell is broken away. Result: eighty-five pounds of flour (over three thousand griddle cakes according to my cookbook mathematics).

Oriental Plastic Items

One year on the northern beaches of Graham Island of the Queen Charlotte Islands, thousands of small red plastic toys about three inches long were strewn for miles, probably a shipload of toys lost from a Chinese freighter. Needless to say, all the children of the area, including the Haida Indian youngsters, were well supplied with toys.

Japanese fishermen, especially, and other Japanese sailors wear plastic slippers we call thongs or zorries, a fact easily established by the number that land on our beaches, especially in areas where we beachcomb for Japanese glass floats, saki bottles, and wood dunnage. For a while I kept records of our findings on Vancouver Island; the ratio was four thongs per glass float and four glass floats to a saki bottle.

In recent years Pacific Ocean beachcombers have been finding plastic containers of all sorts with Japanese printing on the sides. Japanese fishing vessels are making themselves known by their discards. These plastic detergent containers, pill boxes, galley shelf items, hairdressing containers, and so forth, are practically indestructible.

This new plastic bottle is one of the many containers beachcombed
along Pacific coastal shores. Here is a sake container from the Okura
Sake Corporation of Kyoto, Japan. (Author Photo)

Military Debris

World War II Debris

World War II in the Pacific Ocean involved so many men and so
much equipment that debris is still to be found on some beaches. Although much of the seaborne military equipment lies at the bottom of
the ocean, beaches of some island groups like the Marianas and the
Carolines still show and uncover leftover evidence of this massive
struggle. The four hot spot beaches of North America (Port Heiden,
Alaska; Graham Island, British Columbia; Nehalem Spit, Oregon;
and Baja, Mexico) all have periodically amassed buoyant war-related
items such as shipboard mops, airplane pieces, naval mines, electronic
equipment boxes, Mae West jackets, Navy emergency rations, and
supplies. This is not to imply that the Pacific Ocean was polluted by
World War II. It merely means that many such interesting items have
been, are being, and are yet to be beachcombed.

This World War II naval mine was found by Dick Hamlin in southeastern Alaska while looking for Japanese glass floats (above, left). (Dick Hamlin Photo)   Japanese mine washed up on Montague Island, Alaska. (above, right) (Walter Pich Photo)

Beachcombers usually are the first to discover World War II migrant mines that, after having ridden for years in the great Kuroshio Current, are driven upon some Pacific Ocean shore. The United States Navy and Coast Guard keep track of this problem, but occasionally these lethal floating vagabonds of the Pacific conflict are beached. The authorities should immediately be informed. Such mines are dangerous. A later chapter on safety will tell how to avoid this and other beach dangers.

Objects from Airplane Crashes

Aircraft, large transports, or small private planes that crash into the Pacific break up into parts, many of which are buoyant. These pieces are carried by ocean currents to beaches thousands of miles from the scene of the accident; principally, the Japanese Kuroshio Current is responsible for the beaching of airplane parts all the way from Alaska to Baja.

As a rule, the wing and body structure pieces usually sink and stay put. Smaller aircraft that have been ditched successfully often sink intact, depending on conditions. Several Navy fighter aircraft have recently been found off Hawaii in fair condition after submersion for over twenty-five years.

Seat cushions, life vests, oxygen bottles, landing gear wheels, plastic interior parts, tubing, wooden propellors, fuel tanks, oil tanks, sandwich constructed floors, rudders, flaps, and even whole tail portions are the items most often found. Usually this debris can be identified. But aircraft parts found years after the accident are seldom vital to an accident investigation, and there is no Federal Aviation Authority regulation that requires submittal of beachcombed aircraft parts to the government.

Money—and Other Metal Objects

Coins have a way of getting lost into the Pacific Ocean. Because of their flat shape, under surface currents will bury them at one location for a while, later uncovering them and sending them shoreward. Beachcombers may find the occasional coin, such as the 1945 penny found on an isolated sandy beach in Alaska and the five-dollar gold piece found on a gravel beach near Clallam Bay, Washington—both of which had washed in from deeper waters. Chinese coins with square holes in the center were beachcombed by Clatsop Indians before 1800. The coins could possibly be from an oriental vessel shipwrecked off the Columbia River in about 1750. A medallion was found in the 1930s on a western beach of Vancouver Island confirmed as one Captain Cook gave to a Nootkan Indian chief in 1778. Found in 1970 enmeshed in some beached kelp on Vancouver Island was a long piece of cord that had a Union of South Africa coin tied at one end.

Heavily populated and frequented public bathing beaches above the high tide line are the scene of many a lost valuable. Coins and jewelry lost in the sand at such beach areas have been found with the use of the portable metal detector.

Closeup, about four times actual size, of front and reverse of Chinese coin worn by Clatsop Indian woman in 1900. It is believed that many such coins were beachcombed or salvaged by earlier Indians from the wreck of an oriental ship near the mouth of the Columbia River in about 1750. (Burford Wilkerson Photo)

Friends tell of finding a number of dollar bills in good shape on the beach of a lowland lake in central Oregon. The bills came from a billfold that was found opened up a short distance offshore in clear water. An identification card gave the name of the owner. When the person was contacted, he indicated that he had lost it three months before when fishing. He was especially grateful for its return since he had cashed his payroll check just prior to the loss.

There is the story about a special collection of World War I Navy anchors at Poulsbo, Washington. It seems that after World War I a number of wooden ships were berthed in the bay near

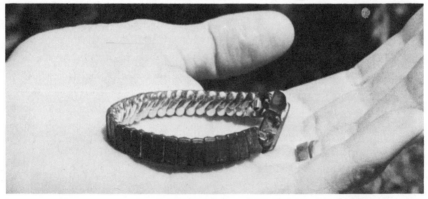

This wristwatch was beachcombed eighteen months after it had been lost in a Washington lake.

Poulsbo, all anchored side by side in a row. When it became necessary to take these ships away, the anchors with some anchor chain were cut loose and left behind. A Poulsbo resident, as a small boy, had remembered all about this. As a middle-aged man, after his discharge from Navy duty following World War II, he decided he would try to locate and salvage those old anchors, knowing that they would have considerable value. He bought a small surplus Navy landing craft and started to drag with grapples for the old anchor chains. With relatively little effort he soon hooked onto a piece of chain and pulled it in as far as he could with the equipment he had aboard. Since the anchor itself was well silted over by then, he cinched up the chain to his craft in such a fashion that he let the action of the tides slowly loosen the anchor. In time he was able to salvage all the anchors, which he then sold at a good profit.

A large, metal object of strange shape was trucked to and displayed by a beachcomber at a recent Seaside, Oregon, beachcomber fair. It was not until after the fair that it was identified as a spent Soviet naval mine.

Huge brass cannons cast in Manila in 1803 were salvaged from early sailing ship rock ballast dumped overboard alongside the wharf at Port Townsend, Washington according to reports.

Pottery

Earthenware containers are generally subject to rapid deterioration, especially when left to the elements; however, where such containers are sealed and have a glazed protective exterior they have been known to resist the ravages of the elements for some time—even being attacked by the Pacific. About two dozen earthenware jugs that have been beachcombed on the Washington and Oregon coasts are believed to have oriental origin. Where they came from, how they were used, and why they were empty are all questions yet to be answered. That they survived the beaching trip through the surf is in itself a small wonder. I have examined a number of these strange-looking earthenware jugs and find them to be of different shapes, stand about twenty inches tall, and weigh about twelve pounds. Recently one of these beachcombed jugs that had been out of the water about five years began to crumble.

Oriental mystery jug beachcombed on the Oregon coast carries the name of the manufacturer in Chinese (above, left).   When this mystery jug was sighted, it was covered with barnacles and was riding low in the water, giving it the appearance of a spent bomb (above, right).
(Ray Gueffroy Photo)

One explanation of their presence on this side of the Pacific is that an oriental junk years ago sank on the Columbia River Bar, and its wreckage was covered by the sands. In time, as these sands shifted, the wreckage was uncovered and these sealed jugs were set free to bob to the surface and be beached at the whims of the tide and wind. To the best of my knowledge, no unglazed unsealed pottery has ever made it across the Pacific to land on this side.

Historical and Anthropological Artifacts

In the Pacific Northwest, Indian artifacts are often found along the beaches. Many small private collections are in existence all along the coast, but probably the most significant and extensive collection is on display at the museum at Neah Bay, Washington.The collection comes from the Ozette Indian Village site at Cape Alava, Washington, which has been dedicated as an archeological site. Over 4,000 artifacts have been uncovered from a series of early mud slides that covered the Indian beach houses of the Ozettes. Some of the artifacts, apparently washed down by the rains over the years, had been discovered in tidal beach areas. A Nootkan war club was dug up by a Boy Scout while digging for clams.

Remains of Indian dugout found on Bayocean peninsula, Tillamook, Oregon. (Burford Wilkerson Photo)

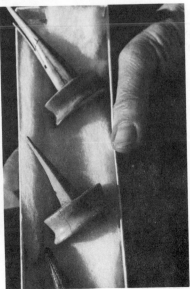

Tray of early Aleutian native ivory carvings found by Doris Cowden in a kitchen midden on the Aleutian chain (above, left).   Closeup of very rare lip labrets that were worn by early Aleutian native women (above, center).   Closeup of ivory talisman figurine found by Doris Cowden (above, right).

Necklace made of rare brown glass Indian trading beads found on sandy saltwater beaches of Port Angeles, Washington (above, left).   Two early Aleutian native fishing sinkers beachcombed near Nelson Lagoon, Alaska (above, center).   Stone scrapers formerly used by Alaskan natives to scrape meat away from the bones of animals that had been killed for food (above, right).

At a spot near Seaside, Oregon, on the Necanicum River, a beachcomber found two flat rocks decorated with unusual markings. An outline of a fish that could have been a salmon or trout was carved on one; on the other was a five-pointed star and the number 1810. The latter marking was probably made by one of the British fur trappers who were located throughout the Oregon Territory in the early nineteenth century. Marked boulders dating back a century or so are not uncommon and also can be traced to early fur traders. The Northwest Company, later named the Hudson's Bay Company, had extensive operations throughout Washington, Oregon, and British Columbia, and these fur traders were in the habit of carving the dates of their activity in stone.

Petroglyphs, as inscriptions on rocks are called, carved by earlier generations of coastal Indians are found on the Pacific Ocean beach at Cape Alava, Washington. At Manzanita, Oregon, near the Pacific Ocean front, are strange unidentified marks on rocks, long believed to contain the secret of the Neahkahnie Mountain treasure. Indian history has it that Spanish sailors from a galleon buried a treasure there. Whatever their true meaning, petroglyphs can be valuable finds for the beachcomber.

The constant action of the surf on Pacific Ocean beaches will bring in sand beds and move them out on a seasonal basis, so historical and anthropological items can continue to be found.

Galleon Debris

For some time now on the Oregon coast, beachcombers have found pieces of Spanish Manila galleon cargos believed to have been deposited there either by shipwreck or the Japan Current. Timbers believed to be from a galleon have been located on the Baja coast. Cargo lost from Manila galleons during storms may have been the first man-made flotsam to drift in Pacific Ocean currents for beaching on our western shores. Prior to this there may have been the occasional oar, canoe, basket, or weapon that floated for great distances; however, the chances of their being found were quite small when compared to the quantity of galleon debris spread around.

Manila galleon trade across the Pacific began in 1565 and continued until 1815. Annual trips were made from Manila to New Spain

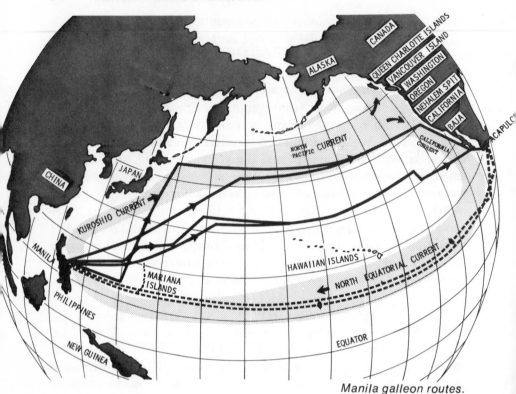

Manila galleon routes.

at Acapulco, Mexico. This amazing operation involved a fleet of ships making voyages that lasted from three to seven months in duration. In all, some thirty-six galleons came to grief. Portions of these vessels, their cargos, even demasted ships were known to have circulated in the Japan Current.

During the ten-year period from 1630-1640 the shipyard at Cavite, Manila, was able to turn out one new galleon each year, roughly the rate of galleon losses then. With crossings of about 9,000 miles—all on routes continuously fraught with typhoons and gales —it is surprising there were not more losses.

Galleon wreckage might be found on any beach of the Pacific Ocean where other oriental debris is beached. To seek Spanish galleon remains or treasures, the beachcomber should look for large weather-beaten timbers cut from oriental woods. Some of these may have been pushed inland by tidal waves well beyond the high tide line.

NATURAL OBJECTS

On Pacific Ocean beaches there is a second major category of items for the beachcomber to find—namely, those of natural origin, not man-made like those I have been describing. Contributing their fair share of interesting debris to stretches of beach drift are the flora and fauna of the seashore and the marine life from the sea. Inland it is plant and wild life of the lakeshore or riverbank and the inter-facing freshwater habitat. Much of the driftwood and agate found on ocean beaches originated at some upland lake or river. Often the salt-water-borne natural flotsam will travel thousands of miles to a new continent, thanks to the Japanese Kuroshio Current. Trees, plants, rocks, birds, mammals, and fish leave evidence on ocean beaches or freshwater riverbanks that attract the attention of the observant searcher.

Woods

Driftwood

Ocean beaches, lakes, and streams offer driftwood of many sizes, shapes, and textures. Small pieces fit into the palm of one's hand; others stretch across a mantel or stand as tall as the room or garden will allow. We have a worm-eaten log standing on end in our garden that resembles a totem pole. At night with an outdoor light beamed upward, the irregularities and shadows present a striking effect.

A log that beached near the author's cabin on Whidbey Island, Washington.

Sample of wormwood beachcombed near Seaside, Oregon. This type of wood is so sought after by craftsmen that it is often sold by the pound.

Huge Douglas fir logs from the Pacific Northwest were known to drift onto Hawaiian Island beaches and were carved into large canoes. California-grown redwood logs have been unearthed from the sands of Vancouver Island. Drift logs of oriental woods are readily identified by Oregon beachcombers. A log with strange Polynesian carvings is believed to have drifted to the Queen Charlotte Islands in British Columbia to trigger the Haida totem pole art craft.

Roots and Other Small Items

Roots, limbs, eroded planks, teredo-eaten boards, knots, and burls lend themselves to a myriad of possible uses and treatments. Many an impressive table lamp has been made from a gnarled piece of wood sculptured by wind and wave, sand and sea. Thin pieces of branch make up readily into mobiles and wall hangings. Driftwood pieces have been made into toy animals, chairs, seats, steps, and the like. Other pieces are found that already resemble animals, birds, or people's faces, due to natural sculpturing by the wind and surf.

Petrified Wood

There is no limit to the amount of petrified wood that can be beachcombed in the Pacific Northwest. Petrified wood has been found on numerous beaches along the Oregon, Washington, and Alaskan coasts, although it is scarce in British Columbia. Personally, I have seen beautiful pieces of petrified black wood with white grains, as well as myrtle, ginkgo, and cedar. Much petrified wood is also found inland.

Seed Pods

In both the Atlantic and Pacific certain seed pods will be carried by ocean currents from one continent to another. The different pods found along Pacific beaches are relatively few. Perhaps this is due to attrition over the larger distances involved and the different conditions encountered upon arrival. For journeys of many years, the pod has to have high survival characteristics. Some plants of the Hawaiian Islands are believed to have come by sea, but not many. Only a small number of plants and trees in Hawaii are like those found in North America.

Country almond fruit native to Hawaii is found on the Oregon coast. (Charles R. Gunn Photo)

Petrified oyster shell beachcombed from the south side of the Aleutian chain near Sand Point, Alaska.

In the Hawaiian Islands when a storm tosses a coconut up onto a higher level of the beach, the coconut will root and another coconut palm will be added to the seashore. Coconuts make their way to western American shores, both with and without husks.

One seed pod that travels the Pacific Ocean currents is the country almond fruit, a peach-like fruit with an outer skin, fleshy interior, and an almond-like pod or stone. Inside the pod is the seed, which tastes and looks like an almond. Native to Hawaii, this seed has been found in Oregon, a 11,100-mile, seven-year journey by Kuroshio. Other tropical seeds may be awaiting identification while lodged in the driftwood on North American ocean shores.

Shells

For the beachcomber who wants to collect shells, the seashore of the Pacific is a veritable paradise. There are mussels from rocky shores, clams from sandy beaches, and oysters from flat tidelands. Other shells, such as scallops and abalone, come from deep water and are beached after storms. It is a rare beach that does not have at least several varieties of shells showing along the high tide line where the surf and latest tides have deposited them.

Some of the common shells of edible mollusks that abound on

This random collection of shells was beachcombed around the Pacific Ocean from Hawaii to British Columbia.

western seashores are the limpet, abalone, moon snail, littleneck clam, cockle, geoduck, horse clam, piddock, razor clam, jackknife clam, pismo clam, butter clam, scallop, oyster, mussel, chiton, and gooseneck barnacle. Other shells, such as sand dollars, are also found by the collector looking for the unusual and exotic; however, the shells mentioned above are the ones most often seen by the beach-comber.

In addition to these shells found from Baja to Alaska, Hawaii adds its own unique species of shells. Found on these islands are augurs, miter, cones, cowries, murex, spindles, triton, horns, strombs, pukas, and others.

Fossils

Fossils of shellfish and plant life are found on Pacific Ocean beaches from California to Alaska, showing beachshore life that was in existence millions of years ago. One such area is Beverley Beach campground in Oregon, where marine life fossils of snails, clams, shells, and scallops are found in relative abundance.

When hunting for fossils, a good place to start is in the layered sandy banks along rivers or in the steep bluffs along the seashore. Clam shell fossils are usually embedded in silt rock layers; when the rock is broken open, the imprints of the shells will be exposed. Many smaller shell fossils the size of a quarter are also found in these rocks, some shaped like a cockle, limpet, triton, or snail. The finds are not limited to shells, however; the imprint of a small fish about four inches long was beachcombed in Washington.

Fossil finds can be spectacular. A small boy picking away at the side of a cliff with a stick let out a call for his father. Between the two of them they removed, intact, an agatized turtle, about twelve inches across the shell.

Rocks

Because there is an endless, ever-present supply of ocean gravel beds, Pacific beach rocks are popular items to beachcomb. Most Pacific beaches contain a wide variety of rock sizes, shapes, and colors. Any rock may be of value to the beachcomber—from those as small as marbles to those as large as can be readily transported. The colorful rocks found in beach gravel range from black to white, with virtually any color in between. Many rocks are variegated, others will contain layered patterns. Since the gravel beds on Pacific Ocean beaches are continually being turned over by the action of surf and tides, there is a continual supply of colorful rocks for the beachcomber to sort through.

Beach rocks are beachcombed for a number of uses. Beach rocks that contain a mixture of colors are sought after for polishing and display; many a glass jar filled with assorted colored rocks adorns the mantels of fireplaces of Pacific coastal homes. Flat, rounded beach rocks are collected solely for their shape, having been ground to that unique shape by some mysterious combination of seashore circumstances. These rocks are used in patio and garden landscaping. If you have access to a cobble beach, you will find rocks that are all nearly spherical in shape and the size of oranges. Where other conditions exist, the rocks may be flat with holes bored through them—ideal for making jewelry. Still other rocks of elliptical shape no bigger than a

These rocks beachcombed from Pacific shores contain borings in the shape of clams.

This boulder, found on Vancouver Island, has been ground to a spherical shape by the action of glacial runoff waterfalls.

Samples of pumice found on Pacific Northwest coastal beaches. Pieces as large as a football were cast up on Washington beaches following the eruption of Mt. St. Helens in May 1980. They were carried down the Toutle and Cowlitz Rivers into the Columbia then out into the Pacific. Pumice floats high in the water about like a tennis ball. (Author Photo)

cookie are collected for craft painting of paperweights and conversation pieces. On Vancouver Island, a huge spherical glacial waterfall boulder about three feet in diameter was located, then moved by bulldozer, and is now used as a driveway marker.

Rocks beachcombed in streams can be large. In this context, there is the story of a man who used to go fishing for steelhead in the Thompson River at Spences Bridge, British Columbia. Year after year he would go downstream from the bridge, where he would sit on a particular rock that was flat enough for him to spread out his lunch. That was his marker point for this particular fishing area. One year he found that "his" rock was gone, though all the others were there as they had been years before. Wondering how such a good-sized rock could disappear, he made inquiries and found that his favorite lunch stop had been hauled away by someone who had recognized it as a large piece of jade and had sold it—for $60,000.

Beach Agates and Jasper

Semiprecious agates—yellow, orange, red, and black—are found in many places along the North American coast, from California into Washington and, to a lesser extent, in British Columbia. The hunting is best in gravel beds in the winter time; in the summer these beds are usually covered over with beach sand many feet thick, thanks to seasonal beach sand shift caused by the differences in the wave size. It

Smokey agate beachcombed near Nelson Lagoon, Alaska (above, left).   Typical selection of beach agates from West Coast shores (above, right).

is believed that beachcombing rockhounds will never exhaust the coastal agate supply—due to the continuous uncovering and burying wave action of the sea—in any event, agate beds can also be found in streams. Some prized agates found on the seacoast are moss, carnelian, rainbow, and cloud. Usually in the same gravel beds, one can find jasper, a kind of quartz that can be white, pink, orange, or black in color.

Ivory

Beachcombed ivory findings are limited principally to the Alaskan beaches; however, occasionally ivory is found along British

Trophy pieces of beachcombed ivory from Nelson Lagoon, Alaska.

Closeup of an expired walrus with the ivory tusks removed. The animal
was found washed up on a beach near Bristol Bay, Alaska. (Dick
Hamlin Photo)

Columbia shores. Tusks from the walrus and teeth from the sperm whale are the principal sources of ivory found on these Pacific beaches. The alert observer may find a piece by spotting a small edge sticking out of the sand. This alertness will certainly pay off since individual sperm whale teeth sell for as high as $100.

Whalebone

Bones of whales are found from Alaska to Baja, and for good reason, since whales beach most anywhere along those shores of the Pacific Ocean. Gray whales migrate that distance, and the sperm, fin, beaked, minke, and killer whale all inhabit the Pacific. At one time, whalebone was in commercial demand for corset stays, but in today's whaling industry the bone skeleton is so much tonnage to be jettisoned. At the present time, whalebone pieces are used as ornaments, and whalebone vertebrae displays always bring admiration.

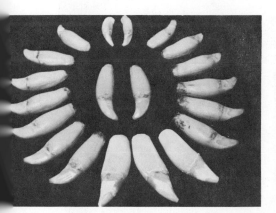

Teeth taken from the lower jaw of sperm whale beached in southeastern Alaska (above, left). (Dick Hamlin Photo)   The narwhal, native only to Icelandic waters, is commercially valued for its ivory tusk. This narwhal, with its eight-foot tusk, was beached at Nelson Lagoon, Alaska, during a storm (above, right). (Doris Cowden Photo)

Beached whales usually stay put, unless near a town whose downwind residents demand removal. At one whale beaching in Oregon, it was necessary to dynamite the carcass into smaller pieces for burial. One large piece of blubber sailed through the air to smash the hood of a parked car, thus incurring an unusual insurance claim.

Spermaceti

Spermaceti, a glistening, waxy substance of light orange color believed to be connected with the whale's buoyancy apparatus, is produced in the huge head cavity of the sperm whale. Commercially it is used in ointments, cosmetics, and candles. A 165-pound tubful of spermaceti was beachcombed on the Oregon coast north of Florence in 1969.

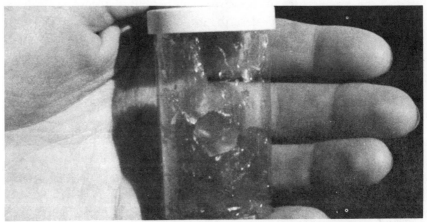

Sample of beachcombed spermaceti taken from a 165-pound find near Florence, Oregon.

Ambergris

Much has been written in the past about the whalers who looked for ambergris and the fabulous prices this wax-like substance brought to the finder. In 1880, at the height of the whaling period, ambergris was more valuable than gold, and in 1948 it was worth eight times the price of gold. Ambergris was so valued because of its unique use as a fixative agent in the manufacture of perfume. It has also been reported to be a powerful aphrodisiac. In ancient China, ambergris was used for medicinal and ceremonial purposes. In 1295 Marco Polo reported beachcombing of ambergris on islands off the coast of India and Madagascar. There is an Ambergris Cay off the coast of British Honduras and one in the Bahamas.

Ambergris only grows in the large intestine of sperm whales. It has been found by whalers at the scene of the catch, has been obtained from the carcass on the deck of a whaling factory ship, and in

The jaw bones, complete with teeth, from a fifty-foot sperm whale and a vertebra from a one-hundred-foot blue whale were both beachcombed on the Queen Charlotte Islands. (Neil Carey Photo)

rare cases has been found drifting in the open sea.

Although it has seldom been discovered by beachcombers, the Queen Charlotte Islands of British Columbia were the scene of a good find in June 1946. This piece apparently drifted into the Japanese Kuroshio Current from more southern latitudes. In 1956, a similar find of fifteen pounds of ambergris sold for $26,000.

It can be assumed that ambergris could be found anywhere around the Pacific Ocean; however, few people in recent years have seen ambergris to properly describe its condition and appearance after it has been adrift for a period of months or years. The sample I examined was charcoal grey or ash colored, but ambergris might be mottled in appearance, similar to the color pattern of the feathers of birds. It can vary from the extremes of almost white to brown or black—one fourteen-pound piece found in Oregon was a yellowish amber color. Pieces could be as small as an egg or as heavy as 900 pounds. It could be expected to be irregular in shape, possibly having the external appearance of a cauliflower. The key item to look for is the pointed beaks of squid that can be seen embedded on the surface. Ambergris is lighter than water and has the specific gravity of wax. It has a pungent, earthy odor—when found, one piece retained a foul stench for a considerable period.

When something is found that has these physical characteristics, the next step is to give it the needle test. Heat an average-sized needle in a blue flame for about fifteen seconds and stick the head end into the substance one-eighth of an inch deep. Should it tend to melt around the needle and leave fine strings when touched, then the material is ambergris.

Knowing what to look for, the beachcomber may add to the legend and lore of this curious substance that travels the Kuroshio.

Beeswax

In 1813 Alexander Henry recorded an Indian visit to the fort at Astoria, Oregon. Among the curiosities he noted were an Indian with red hair and the pieces of beeswax that the Indians brought for trading purposes. Henry learned that the wax came from a location to the south of the Columbia River where a Spanish ship was wrecked. Thus began the saga of the beeswax found in the Oregon beach sands.

Circular piece of beeswax found near South Jetty on Bayocean, Oregon (above, left). (Burford Wilkerson Photo)   Burford Wilkerson displays beeswax on Manzanita Beach near where it was found in 1909 (above, right).

Some of the earlier pieces of beeswax were quite large and appeared to be from slabs as large as twenty-four by sixteen by four inches. It has been estimated that, over the years, literally tons of this wax have been recovered from Oregon beaches. Even in recent years pieces of this wax have been found by beachcombers. This beeswax floats and is quite durable—more so than the Manila galleons that are presumed to have brought it. I have a piece of this beeswax on my desk, and even though it is some three hundred years old, it still gives off a honey sweet odor when sliced with a knife.

The wax is considered to be cargo from a Spanish Manila galleon. Study of records in the archives of Seville has indicated that wax was a deck cargo of eastbound galleons and was destined for candle manufacture. Some of the pieces found had portions of numbers and letters, believed to be identification marks of Manila shippers. The great quantity of wax found on Oregon beaches seems to indicate that the source was a shipwreck near the shore.

Although there has been a great deal of conjecture about the wax and its markings, nothing specific was done until 1961 when Burford Wilkerson of Tillamook, Oregon, arranged to have a sample of this wax carbon-14 dated. The results showed that the wax was made in 1681 plus or minus 110 years. Chemical analysis of a sample indicated that it had come from the Orient. Between 1571 and 1791 there were six galleons lost at sea: the *San Juanillo*, the *San Antonio*, the *San Nicholas*, the *Santo Cristo de Burgon*, the *San Francisco Xavier*, and the *Pilar*. A number of people think that it was the *San Francisco Xavier*, lost in 1705, that may have been wrecked on the Oregon coast, but no definite information is available.

MISCELLANEOUS ITEMS

You can beachcomb *anything*, and people do. Sometimes an ordinary household item is accidentally lost off the coast of Japan—to be tossed, one thousand days later, at the feet of a completely baffled Oregon coastal beachcomber. The joy of the hobby is meeting the unexpected.

In about 1960 a silver ball seven inches in diameter was picked up on the Oregon coast. Its use or purpose has baffled all who have examined it. The ball was sent to the Atomic Energy Commission, and even their staff scientists were puzzled. They did report that it was not an item made or used by the Commission, that the metal shell was one-sixteenth of an inch thick, and that it was made of an alloy containing chromium and nickel.

Volunteers carefully remove dirt from around a locomotive before it is raised by crane from its burial spot at Port Townsend, Washington. (Port Townsend Leader *Photos)*

One of the most exciting finds on a beach area in recent years was that of an old railroad locomotive near Port Townsend, Washington. It was discovered when a small rusty piece of metal was found protruding from the sand—an edge of a railroad wheel. Since this locomotive had been the subject of searches over the past sixty years, news of this discovery spread quickly to local historians and rail buffs. After the earth was carefully dug away from around the locomotive, it was lifted out of its grave with a heavy duty crane and turned over on its wheels.

Books have also shown up on Pacific beaches. In 1903 a log book containing 600 handwritten pages in Spanish was found on the Washington coast. Friends recently found Russian-English and Japanese-English dictionaries on the beach near Florence, Oregon.

All these man-made and natural beachcombed objects comprise a sufficiently comprehensive list to entice almost any person to a Pacific Ocean beach to answer for himself, "What can be found?"

Rare beachcombed item is this buoy light used in nighttime oriental long-line tuna fishery operations around the Pacific Ocean. The metal frame supporting a light at the top is buoyed by large glass float and encased battery below. (Author Photo)

3
Beachcombing Techniques

The beaches of the Pacific Ocean western states may be beachcombed week in and week out, year in and year out. However, for productive results, it is best to concentrate on those beaches that historically have produced drift lines of ocean-borne debris.

General Suggestions and Rules

When you beachcomb:
- Select beaches away from large population centers.
- Pick the more inaccessible beaches, particularly those where driftwood collects.
- Beachcomb during and after storms, especially after sustained periods of onshore winds.
- Beachcomb during and after winter and spring storms rather than summer or fall storms, which generally are of shorter duration.
- Avoid beachcombing during long periods of offshore winds.
- Avoid weekends and vacation periods, especially on easily accessible beaches.
- Concentrate your beachcombing on Thursdays in order to allow

Monday through Wednesday accumulations at the high tide levels.

- Beachcomb at high tide periods, even at night.
- Watch for such "Indian signs" as coincident arrival of driftwood, kelp, and velella.
- Select flat beaches with heavy surf rather than those that are steep.
- Walk the upwind direction on the beach so that the return trip will have a tail wind.

Clothing and Footwear

Clothing

Some people dress up to go beach hiking—others dress down for their beachcombing. It may depend on whether you are a tourist or a local resident. How many people you expect to meet along the way may also dictate the style for that day. When preparing to meet the worst of weather, the style-conscious hiker will want to wear the same type of clothing that he would wear while golfing or boating. Net underwear, woolen slacks and sweater, dacron-lined waterproof hiking pants, jacket, and a rain cap will serve the average person through almost any inclement condition for a few hours, perhaps even for an all-day hike.

Quilted three-quarter length ski jackets are popular. Two-piece rain suits and mariner's suits are practical choices for general beachcombing garb. A lightweight ski parka also serves to go over a medium-weight woolen sweater. A ski cap or a sou'wester is my choice while hiking in a driving rain. For a day-long hike in a continual rain, a poncho is a good selection for outerwear. In general, clothes that are suitable for other marine or hiking recreational activities are also suitable for beachcombing. For winter coastal storms of driving snow and cold rain the wrong combination of clothing can be agonizingly miserable.

It is important to keep the water from running down one's neck, otherwise some of the clothing will get wet on the inside. You should select clothing that gives comfort while you are climbing up rocks and over driftwood, yet keeps you warm during a leisurely walk in a downpour. Bib-type overalls of rain-resistant fabrics make good outer trouser gear as attested to by many a fisherman; the overalls also will keep water from running down into your footwear and stockings.

Wind is the single most consistent weather element on a western Pacific Ocean beach. Close behind is rain. Summer or winter, the ocean wind is to be reckoned with. For thousands of miles no land mass has slowed it down nor disturbed its moisture content. Even at relatively low wind velocities, Pacific Ocean coastal onshore winds have a chill factor that should be taken into consideration when selecting beach wear. In a driving rain, the wind will force water through the smallest of seams in a newly purchased outer garment.

Parkas and trousers made of fabrics with impermeable surfaces may shed the outside rain but will hold both the condensation from the interior surface and the trapped body moisture, which together give a chilling effect. On the other hand, a tight rubberized parka over a loosely knitted raw wool sweater can be comfortably warm on a bright sunny day in the winter when the wind is blowing hard. Even an inexpensive lightweight clear plastic jacket cover makes a good windbreaker. In a strong cold wind the raw wool sweater, alone, will not give complete protection.

For beachcombing in below freezing weather a beachcomber friend, who had previously worked as a railroad brakeman in Montana in the winter in high winds, suggested his proven outfit of long johns, army surplus wool pants and shirt, and an army surplus summer flying suit of fine tightly woven poplin. The external pockets of the flying suit provided ample space for modest-sized beach loot.

For those who dress down for their beachcombing, the oldest and most hideous hand-me-downs are in vogue on any respectable beach. I have seen some disreputable outfits that would not normally be worn into town, unless that town was a small isolated fishing village. Invariably these outfits, which always add a bit of charm to the beach scene, contain woolen clothing that is completely comfortable in a driving rain. I used to think that to be comfortable while beachcombing one should dress as the commercial fishermen do, but those hearty souls seem to have Viking blood in their veins and require fewer clothes to keep warm than most land dwellers.

Some people dress Chinese coolie style for their beachcombing; that is, wearing numerous layers of thin materials, putting on as many layers as may be comfortable for that day. Cotton flannel shirts are fine for this. I have worn four in the dead of winter and felt comfortable. Several layers of trousers also work well, but watch out for the nylon and dacron fabrics. They may appear to be warm, but once they get rainsoaked, they lose their warmth. Likewise, Levis made of cotton denim are not recommended for cold, wet weather. For winter coastal beachcombing weather, there is no satisfactory substitute for woolen clothing. I always make sure I have one layer of wool in my slack and shirt combination.

For headgear, a ski cap or knitted wool stocking cap is ideal for beach hiking. I often wear the red one that my wife knitted for me. She says she can keep track of me a long distance away and know exactly what I am doing. However, I find that this cap is not practical for stream beachcombing or lake beach hiking because it is continually getting caught on bushes or low branches; at those locations, I wear a ski cap.

Almost any season of the year I wear my flannel-lined corduroy parka coat. It zips up the front and ties under my chin when the hood is in place. Although designed as a stadium coat, it has been my multipurpose, many-seasoned, constant beachcombing companion. In its large button-down pockets, I carry lunch, camera, knife, gloves, and other items. I can also fold up my ski cap and slide it into one of the pockets. This coat has seen lots of miles of driftwood hiking and on several occasions has afforded me added protection when I have fallen on a slippery log. I often wear a ski cap with the parka hood over that, which still allows for good lateral visibility.

Regarding clothing for Pacific coastal beachcombing, a summer day in the southern climates is the least demanding, while a winter storm in the northern areas is the most critical of conditions. Considerable beachcombing is accomplished in southern California without a second thought given to protective clothing, only for necessary cover against sunburn. However, the beachcomber who would do his beach hiking north of mid-Oregon will do well to dress properly for the occasion.

Footwear

There is no substitute for foot comfort during a full day of serious beachcombing, and no greater disaster if the wrong footwear is worn. Footgear depends on the location, season, and type of beach to be walked. For example, walking over long distances in shoes with smooth soles in dry loose sand is quite tiring because of the continual slipping. A waffle or lug type sole is a must for loose dry sand in order to keep a firm footing at each step, especially when considering that it will take almost 15,000 steps for a seven-mile beach hike. In sunny climates and wide, hard sandy beaches, low tennis shoes are suitable;

Beachcombed dimension lumber can be carried long distances where beach gravel gives good footing.

Dick Hamlin wears work boots and carries a walking stick to do his beachcombing on the volcanic beach at Port Heiden, Alaska. (Dick Hamlin Photo)

yet for climbing over rocky outcroppings, such as found in Alaska, one will want heavy boots. Even hip boots are handy when it is necessary to ford a series of streams. Knee-high fisherman's boots are splendid where one expects to slosh along at the water line or cross numerous small streams.

When one expects to be doing his beachcombing by climbing over driftwood for most of the day, I recommend an over-the-ankle lightweight work boot for the Pacific Northwest area, which is the best all-around selection for any time of year. For gravel or cobble beaches, a hiking boot or work boot is desirable.

The length of the beach walk may well dictate the choice of footwear. Shoes are *usually* fine for short walks. Many a time I have worn heavy hip boots and wished I had left them home; yet, just as many times, I have come across a two-foot rocky stream and wished I had them along when I had to ford the stream in my bare feet. On a new beach, I will wear hip boots on the outbound trip and change into work boots for the return walk where possible. For a short beach hike on a hard sandy beach when the weather is warm, the pleasure of going barefoot supersedes all other means.

Seasonal Adjustments

Weather Patterns

Beachcombing techniques should be adjusted to seasonal weather patterns. Since our beachcombing takes place between 30° and 60° north latitude of the western Pacific Ocean shoreline, let us review seasonal weather at a near-midway location like Tillamook on the northern Oregon coast.

Here the seasonal weather pattern is as follows. For the winter season there are southwest rain storms often lined up in the Pacific to hit the coast every few days and south winds that drive the seas parallel to shore; prevailing winds at times reach gale velocities. There are overcast weather and low visibility periods; although rainfall is heavy, snow seldom falls. In spring there is a blend of the weather of all seasons, and at intervals the south and southwest winds shift to the west to delight the beachcomber. Summers are cool, rainfall is light, and prevailing afternoon winds are from the northwest. Fall, especially September and October, offers delightful weather—warmer

A gray, bleak scene during a typical Pacific Ocean winter storm on the Oregon coast. Sixty-mile-per-hour winds and heavy rain result in an angry surf and low visibility.

because the northwest winds of summer have subsided.

This means that during the winter season the beachcomber must be on the beach in the fury of a storm and high surf to snatch anything of interest from short-lived tide lines before a change in tide or wind carries everything back into the sea. For springtime beachcombing in the same area, one should watch for the steady westerly winds during less tempestuous seas that send in large Japanese glass fishing floats and other gooseneck barnacle-laden drift. Oftentimes the floats can be spotted in the surf prior to beaching. In the summertime the beachcomber must concentrate his beach hours at the higher tide levels for items like bottles and shells that have been tossed up beyond the line of vegetation during previous winter high tide storms.

In the fall season the beach pickings are slim. There might be some leftovers, but the beachcomber must crisscross the whole wide beach at different levels and cover lots of miles, working hard to glean what he can. Most beaches then have the distinct look of having been well picked over (which they have by the summer beach population) and of having considerable undesirable drift debris underfoot. There are the plastic milk cartons, detergent containers, and lotion dispensers, all waiting for some good Samaritan to pull together into a bonfire. But this seldom happens; the debris usually awaits winter seasonal storms for redistribution, hopefully to another beach some distance away. Not all oriental debris is eagerly sought after by the North American beachcomber, but seasonal weather patterns help in his selection.

Tides

Normal variations in tidal patterns have a rhythmic effect on Pacific coast beachcombing. Again using an Oregon beach location as an example, when tidal changes are small, little new drift appears; when tidal changes are large, considerable new drift shows. When adding tidal effects to normal seasonal storm activity, beachcombing results are affected accordingly. An extremely high tide during a winter coastal storm often spells disaster for the coastline. This combination of elements and its devastation always makes headlines, but conversely provides a multitude of new findings for the alert beachcomber. Minimal tide changes in late summer usually mean a placid, peaceful water's edge—a rare condition—making it easy to launch a small boat into the ocean just to say you have done it at a location where the winter before a high tidal angry surf tossed boom logs around like matchsticks.

During winter seasonal high tides, coastal residents closely watch the weather reports. If there is an offshore wind, they give a sigh of relief, for that may negate the action of the high tide. If, however, an ocean storm hits coincident with a high tide, the coast is due for a drubbing. The onshore winds create an added foot or so to the tide level, flatter land areas are flooded, and high tide beach logs are refloated to be driven by the storm inland into fields and across roads. Summer cottages and small homes built near the water's edge in minutes become victims to this wave and beach log invasion. Other homes further back will have beach drift deposited on the lawn, on doorsteps, and even front porches—a dividend if you own a wood-burning stove. Out on the beaches, the sluing of these logs back and forth is dangerous business. During such a storm I once saw a half-mile long beach lowered one foot overnight, uncovering buried piling stumps not visible the day before. The power of a high tide, onshore winds, combined with a coastal storm and its angry surf is to be respected—preferably observed from a safe distance.

The tide line on a flat sandy Pacific Ocean beach with a rolling surf is a likely place to find Japanese glass floats. (Washington State Parks & Recreation Photo)

The tidal effect on beachcombing is substantial. Additional debris previously deposited along and behind the line of vegetation gets loosened and floats inland with each advancing wave. Many smaller items that had previously been buried in the sand are buoyed about to find new exposed homes at inland locations. Even metal items, such as sailing ship fittings, that had been buried will be exposed on the beaches. Inlets and tidal streams are especially vulnerable to high tides, as they also are to the occasional destructive seiche wave.

Tidal effects on beachcombing are dependent on location along the Pacific coast. The amount of tide is approximately proportional to latitude, meaning that in Hawaii at 20° north latitude there may be a two-foot tide; San Francisco, California, at 38° may have an eight-foot tide; while Anchorage, Alaska, at 61° may have a twenty-foot tide. Thus, depending upon where you may be beachcombing, the season of the year, and the particular tide pattern of a given day, the tidal effects on the beachcombing will be good, bad, or indifferent.

Special Equipment

When your beachcombing means a walk of several hours and miles, there are many useful things that can be taken along that will enhance your beachcombing pleasures. Assuming that the creature comforts are taken care of first—footwear, clothing, headgear, and food (and these four items are needed whether you are on a sunny tropic isle or on a snowblown Aleutian inlet)—you should seriously consider adding many of the following items in your pursuit of a specialized beachcombing activity.

A small rucksack will enable you to carry what you want to bring home. This will not hamper your climbing nor hinder your walking. If you are expecting to carry back fifty pounds or more of beach trophies, then you will want something larger, perhaps a lightweight backpack. My wife always takes along a small plastic bag to carry back the shells she picks up. When the Japanese glass fishing floats are coming, many a person has taken off his jacket and used it as a large sack to carry back these prizes. A beachcomber at Seaside, Oregon, once took off his long underwear to use as a sack, so many glass balls were available for the picking.

The second most useful item to acquire is a walking stick for climbing rocks and driftwood. A staff the size of a broom handle is ideal. If you expect to beachcomb where the driftwood is scarce and a good walking stick is apt not to be found from the beach drift itself, then bring along an old ski pole. There is nothing to give better security while cruising atop the driftwood in the rain than a lightweight ski pole.

On occasion I have carried a small metal rod about two feet long in my rucksack to probe sand banks. It is mighty handy for that time when a glass float is seen in a vertical sand bank at the edge of the sea, and you know there are others buried nearby.

The rockhound beachcomber will want to add a prospector's hammer to his gear to break open rocks for inspection. The agate beach hunter will add a sieve and shovel in his knapsack. I know a beach rock comber who got tired of continually stooping down to pick up beach rocks, so she took an inexpensive kitchen serving spoon, bent up the spoon end, and added a longer handle, enabling her to select rocks for closer inspection without bending over.

A regular shovel is much too heavy for beachcomber use unless your objective is to dig razor clams, in which case you would want a clam gun, a special long-necked, short-handled digger. For most general digging purposes, a small army surplus shovel is an ideal item to pack. Since agate beds sometimes get covered over with sand, the shovel will be useful for the selective digging and screening that will

Razor clam digger is persistent as wave rushes in to cover up digging operation near Ocean Park, Washington. (Hjalmar Brenna Photo)

be necessary. I have even packed a trowel to dig out items that I had seen on a previous hike, but never have I taken such heavy digging tools as a spade.

A boy scout hatchet is lightweight and will be useful in removing driftwood branches and other debris. For larger pieces of wood, such as cedar logs, it may be more useful to carry a small hand saw. However, if you intend to use a saw, the sawing must be done on clean, dry wood; otherwise the beach sand will dull the saw in a few minutes time.

When metal fittings, bolts, or spikes are to be salvaged from timbers or ship wreckage, carry along crescent wrenches, screwdrivers, and a small can of oil. Two of my own beachcombing experiences demonstrate the usefulness of these tools. Once I found a fishing boat pilothouse that had washed up onto the driftwood after a storm. On the outside, it had two handrails bolted on below the side window frames. A month later I returned with some wrenches in my knapsack and salvaged both handrails, which today serve as towel racks in our saltwater beach cabin at Whidbey Island, Washington.

On another occasion I needed two dozen large tie bolts about twenty inches long for use in a concrete bulkhead I was constructing at my home. Thanks to extensive timber drift that was brought in by winter storms, I was able to beachcomb all the needed bolts in a relatively short time. I obtained several bolts by driving beachcombed wooden wedges into the ends of the planks, splitting the ends just wide enough to allow the bolt to fall free. The salvage of bolts and fittings from beach drift is an ingenious craft and of considerable use when a specific requirement is to be met, but a great waste of time when no needful purpose is at hand.

Basic Techniques

Scanning

Effective and continuous scanning is the key to good beachcombing.

If several parallel drift lines are spread out on a flat beach, it is best to walk up the beach searching the most recent tide line or the one nearest the water. Then, walking back down the beach, search the highest tide line or the one nearest the land vegetation. However you choose to walk, your visual scanning techniques will play a big part in locating the various drift items that are beached. Looking about in a

When beachcombing a wide drift-strewn beach area, look down into nooks and crevices for smaller objects that are packaged in place by the action of high tides.

Considerable effort is sometimes required to remove a long piece of Japanese wood when other logs are jammed on top.

A five-inch Japanese float photographed as it might be found.

random fashion may be pleasant, but this process can only cover the beach in a random pattern. Many a person has walked past such prizes as shiny Japanese glass fishing floats lying on a flat beach during a bright day because he has not been looking or scanning the beach surface in an effective manner.

Scan alternately *three* general areas at *three* different distances: immediately ahead, within six feet; at sixty feet; and at one hundred yards. Do *not* concentrate on any one single distance; by doing so, you run the risk of missing items at the other ranges. If you turn around occasionally to look back at the area you have walked, you often note items that you have missed because of the sun's position, shadows, or overcast conditions.

Proper scanning techniques are more important than one might think at first, because even the pay-dirt area of an interesting beach will often be a hundred or more feet wide, and this is a relatively narrow belt on a broad beach that may well exceed eight hundred feet from low tide to the vegetation line.

Watching for Signs

The next important basic technique for beachcombers to learn is that of recognizing the many indicators that foretell good or bad beachcombing conditions. "Indian signs" often give advance notice that portend a change in the weather. Highly visible cloud formations continually reflect meteorological changes that directly affect the tidal zone. The direction of the wind at a particular beach, as well as strong winds out over the open sea, should be noted. Seasonal regularity of

When kelp has been washed ashore after a storm, the beachcomber can usually anticipate a number of other treasures.

these happenings will aid the beachcomber—unseasonal shifting of the wind or ocean currents must be studied to predict the more favorable beaching conditions. The arrival of sea inhabitants or birds at a beach relate to conditions that will affect the beachcombing. All of these signs might be called beachcomber barometers.

Velella Lata. One of the better known beachcomber barometers that arrives from the sea is a two-inch long blue jellyfish with a white sail named *velella lata,* called velella for short. These floating jellyfish are observed by beachcombers from British Columbia to California. Their mass stranding may leave a light blue jelly mass along the high tide line, which on occasion creates a walking hazard due to the extreme slipperiness of the residue. However, once these creatures are left on the beach in the sun, the velella dries in a few days to a translucent paper-like marine castaway.

According to sightings by coastal residents over a thirty-year period, these strange coelenterates of the open sea usually arrive during the winter months. The arrival of velella on western Pacific Ocean beaches has also presaged beachings of Japanese glass fishing floats, and the association of the two is well known on the coast. I had earlier concluded that the first items to beach would be those with the lowest water drag for a given sail area. During a late winter storm at the beach with an onshore wind, the sequence of beachings has also

Closeup of velella lata.

The arrival of velella is closely associated with the beaching of glass floats.

been observed to be: velella, big floats, planks and logs, small floats, kelp, and finally roller floats.

At least this was the general sequence until the mid-1960s when resident beachcombers began to notice changes in the rhythms and patterns of the sea. Something was going on within the ocean currents that was not readily understood—winter storms did not develop, velella were not seen, glass floats did not show, and the beaches were clean of drift.

Early in the 1970s velella started to appear in August along British Columbia and Washington shores. This time their arrival was not at the height of southwest coastal storms, but, instead, in summer weather. When I first saw velella on Vancouver Island beaches in August, I shook my head. A few days later I observed them on a calm ocean two miles offshore. Concurrent with my Canadian sightings, charter and commercial fishermen were also sighting velella and netting glass floats—some five miles off the Washington coast.

At the time I felt that this unusual summer stranding of the velella was telling us that there were problems elsewhere in the Pacific. In any event, the appearance of the rectangular jellyfish with the triangular white sail on top is always good news for the beachcomber. A study of the wanderings of velella may someday explain why it is one of the better beachcombing signs.

Wind Signs. Beach wind direction, velocity, and duration has a great deal to do with beachcombing success, although it is not an absolute guarantee of results. For wind direction, an onshore wind is to be preferred over an offshore wind. Onshore winds perpendicular (normal) to the beach are productive, while winds parallel to the beach are generally nonproductive. Quartering winds to the beach may yield drift depending upon wind velocity and local geography. Many beaches that curve out into the ocean to form a peninsula will catch ocean drift in a quartering wind, while other peninsular areas that might appear to be good drift catchers will have the drift beached on the lee shore rather than on the windward side. Thus, although wind direction is an important beachcombing barometer, it must be considered together with other factors.

Onshore winds at or above fifteen miles per hour are usually productive, while winds below that velocity are apt not to be. Productive quartering winds must be at or above twenty-three miles per hour, while gale winds along the western Pacific coast may usually be of lesser velocity than onshore winds.

Wind *duration* must also be noted. It has been theoretically determined that it takes a steady wind of at least fifteen miles per hour, almost perpendicular to the beach, and with a minimum duration of fifteen hours for ocean waves to send ocean drift ashore. This study done by Frank Kistner in Oregon is supported by beachcombing experience up and down the coast. Increased direction of quartering winds with higher velocities still seem to require the fifteen hours to produce drift. Many a coastal beachcomber has watched favorable conditions build up only to see these change a few hours short of the fifteen-hour period, which concurrently changes his outlook from expectation to disappointment.

Tide Signs. By watching the tide line, the beachcomber can learn a great deal about beachcombing conditions. It doesn't matter whether the tide is coming in or going out—there are signs that tell what is happening. Often when the tide is coming in, small bits of kelp ends will line the beach. This is a good sign; it means the kelp further out is being churned up by the surf with an onshore flow action. If large batches of kelp are washed in, excellent beachcombing conditions exist; some large recent disturbance has torn the kelp from its ocean floor attachment. If there are bits of wood and bark with rounded-off ends along the tide line, that is a bad sign; these bits of wood that have been thrown about in the wave action have probably come from the shoreline of a previous high tide. If lines of foam are along the tide line, this is a good sign meaning that the surf action is high. Debris will be deposited within the foam, and many a glass fishing float has been discovered within the tidal beach foam. Boom logs or large planks lining the tide line are also good signs, since only large onshore forces bring them in.

Coastal Weather Signs. Weather and weather patterns are of great concern to the beachcomber. Many weather signs relate to what will happen at coastal areas, and weather patterns spell out the direction of beachcombing opportunities. The old saying, "a red sunset at night is a sailor's delight," is certainly true for the western Pacific coast. This observation usually foretells clear weather with a steady wind. Sun dogs, hazy spots located to each side of the sun in a thin overcast sky in the late afternoon, announce deteriorating weather and rain for the following day. Both of these are examples of global weather signs. Some weather signs are regional, others are local. An example of a regional weather sign is the overcast level, high or low, on a particular day. A local weather sign might be a revolving wave pattern around a point of land that extends into the ocean.

Some believe that successful beachcombing depends on the wind, which in turn builds up ocean waves, the result of massive air movements over water. Others contend the opposite—the ocean itself generates and determines the weather above its surface. Scientific literature has started to include material that explains that a new pattern of weather, which has been experienced across North America, is now believed to be caused by changing ocean water temperature patterns in the Pacific Ocean. During 1970 and 1971, the central Pacific became warmer and the eastern Pacific waters became cooler, which affected the jet stream wind pattern, which in turn determined continental weather. It is not known what caused the shift in ocean water temperatures nor how long the present temperature patterns will continue. Perhaps this is tied to the melting Arctic ice cap and sunspot activity cycles.

Even before the scientific evidence had been published, beach hikers had known for several years that beachcombing had been unusually poor. All of the coastal weather signs were negative—either the ocean weather was on a new schedule or the ocean currents had changed. At this point it is difficult to consider ocean weather matters without mentioning ocean current effects.

It was feared by some beachcombers that the Kuroshio Current was not following its accustomed route. Other beachcombers believed that glass fishing floats and other drift items were not being beached because glass floats were not being manufactured anymore. Nothing could be further from the truth. A considerable number of floats are produced each year and lost to the Pacific. If anything, the reserve of glass floats still riding Pacific currents is increasing. My calculations indicate that there are about 12,000,000 strung out around in the northern Pacific Ocean merely waiting to be cast ashore with suitable weather conditions.

More disturbing than the absence of glass floats was the fact that none of the Phase III Citizen wristwatch buoys had ever been reported, nor had a single one of the 3,000 plastic drift envelopes been found. These had been released off the coast of northern Japan as a part of a Kuroshio Current survey. They should have arrived

Side view of the Friendship wristwatch buoy shows the way it rides in the water.

Friendship letter buoy has plastic foam flotation strip at the top and a small metal rod enclosed at the bottom.

along the Pacific Northwest coast in 1967, but didn't—they, too, could still be circling in the ocean currents. Numerous earlier cases of bottles containing messages made the same trip from northern Japan, arriving on Oregon beaches in about 1,100 days.

Other strange happenings were reported. Northern California coastal waters had gotten warmer. Unexplained high tides off the eastern coast of Japan were traced to a shift of the Kuroshio Current near their coast. Hearing this, beachcombers assumed that the Pacific coast ocean currents had moved out to sea, and in some mysterious fashion, oriental drift was now completely bypassing coastal beaches.

I had expected casual shifting of major Pacific Ocean currents, but I was not prepared for the major changes in weather patterns discovered by the scientists. They found that high-altitude jet stream patterns had shifted and had affected the weather across the nation. Storms were now approaching our western coast at a southern latitude, at such places as southern California, rather than at such northern latitudes as Washington.

The concern over this new development was of sufficient importance that a jointly funded government program called NORPAX (North Pacific Experiment) was undertaken. This study will bring together an interdisciplinary team of oceanographers and meteorologists, two groups who have seldom collaborated before. This team is embarking on an investigation to determine the relationship between ocean water temperature and long-range weather forecasting. This is good news for everyone, especially the Pacific beachcomber. What will be considered the norm in the global picture of ocean currents, and their effect in generating Pacific coastal weather, will also be used to understand day-by-day beachcombing results in terms of local weather conditions and weather signs.

Ocean Current Signs. The beachcomber from his sea-level walkway behind the surf cannot see the wanderings of ocean currents; however, occasionally when the sea is flat, surface drift can be seen traveling with surface currents. From a higher bluff, the confluence of river into ocean, local maelstroms, and coastwise lateral flow can be observed. Observing the way that drift is held in the eddies, how turbulence spreads it out, and why tide rips change everything, will help explain the probable travelings of ocean drift as it approaches our coast.

On those rare occasions when the sea is flat, climb a bank or sand dune to a higher vantage point, drive a couple of sticks into the soil as sighting markers, and watch the lateral drift on the ocean surface. The coastwise Davidson Current changes direction seasonally and thereby affects coastal beachcombing results. It has been observed that beachcombing is poor when this current is flowing north; when it is heading south, beachcombing is good. One time on Vancouver Island when the ocean was extremely quiet, glass fishing floats were seen about two miles out in a long line parallel to the shore.

Drift bottle experiments are continually adding to the knowledge of surface current travel. The effects of the Japanese Kuroshio Current on coastwise currents and drift travel is profound. The exact sequence of factors that cause a saki bottle, tossed into the sea off northern Japan, to land on a California beach is not readily explained.

Although it might be helpful to understand the precise nature of this major current, the principal ocean current that the beachcomber ought to watch and try to understand is the boundary layer shore current that is immediately beyond the surf. In the last analysis, this is the current that finally counts in transporting open ocean drift for shorebound surf delivery.

Surface current patterns in bays, inlets, straits, and sounds are readily observed and the drift can be easily tracked, but tidal considerations override the local pattern to carry such drift to other locations. In such waters this water-borne drift can be searched while drifting about in a small boat.

Shore Birds. Another barometer of beachcombing conditions is the presence of birds. The sea gull with his ravenous appetite continuously haunts the beach in search of food; when the surf is bringing in sea life, he is there to get his share. The sandpiper runs just ahead of a wave as it advances and behind it as it recedes, picking off tidbits along the way. The osprey dives into the breaking surf snatching sea perch on the wing, then soars away. I have seen an eagle pick up a small salmon from the surface of the sea and fly to a nearby beach. I have followed a snowy owl at night in the fog, watching it beachcomb the high tide line for food.

The presence of birds at the beach usually means good foraging opportunities. Whatever brings about feeding conditions for the birds, such as a high surf grinding away at the edibles in the tidal zone, also brings in ocean-borne debris of interest to man. The opposite is also true; a beach that does not attract birds usually is not a good beach-combing spot. Migrations of birds and fowl often occur when winds are favorable in the direction of their destination, so the northerly or southerly winds during those times mean poor beachcombing.

Special Techniques

Freshwater Lakes and Streams

The special beachcombing techniques to be used on the beaches of inland lakes and streams are related to the different geography encountered. Some lakes are in relatively flat land with wide beaches, few trees, and little brush. Others are in foothill areas with steep banks, trees, and brush up to the very edge of the water. Some streams are placid, winding watercourses with an occasional sandbank; others cascade down a mountain side at a fast clip. Thus, there are different conditions and methods suggested for covering a variety of beach terrains.

Lakes. The lakes that are in flat, arid country are readily walked around and usually provide little challenge. Lakes that are in locales that have an average annual rainfall of 20-40 inches are usually bounded by considerable undergrowth, with brush growing up to the water's edge and limbs of trees hanging out over the water. Traditionally the fishermen have long since made a trail around most lakes, but considerable brush fighting is still required to get to all the shore areas. In coastal regions where the annual rainfall will exceed 100 inches, inland lakes are often littered with deadfalls—so be prepared for lots of climbing. The big difference between hiking an inland lake and an ocean beach is the greater amount of effort that is required to make headway through the brush and fallen trees around the lake.

Lake beaches are neither very long nor very wide; although beaches along a saltwater ocean shore may be miles in length and 600 feet wide, one must be content with inland lake beaches of 100 yards long and six feet wide. Lake beaches consist of sand, rock, gravel, clay, and bog; in other words, there is more variety of shore that will be encountered at a lake than on the ocean.

In lake beachcombing the principal problem is access to short stretches of beach separated by brush. The most productive lakeshore beachcombing has been accomplished by using a small boat. This way any overhanging limbs are avoided and access to the next beach is readily gained. It is certainly easier to row short distances than to continuously fight the brush. Also, if you find any heavy pieces of artistic driftwood, you can easily transport them over long distances. A makeshift raft would do, but considerable time is required to construct a raft of available logs, and the poling of the raft from one spot to another is time consuming, particularly if there is any wind.

For the thick brush that you will encounter, take special precautions by wearing sunglasses and a cap with a bill to protect your face. Protection against wind is of no special concern.

Most lakes have variable and seasonal lake levels that change the shore edge. When lakes are high, usually in the spring, they extend up into the sod and vegetation. When they are low, usually in late summer, the extended sun-baked shore bottoms do not produce much of interest.

It is important to establish where the high lake levels have been because anything tossed up at that level is apt to stay until the next high water mark takes place. Always determine the direction of the prevailing winds during the high lake level, because much of what is cast adrift on the lake is going to sail downwind.

Don't limit yourself to searching the beach areas; drift also collects in marshy areas with reeds and cattails. Here, again, a small boat is useful when searching such areas.

The actual searching is much the same as for an ocean beach, but is completed in surprisingly quick order for these smaller beaches. There are no tidal considerations and no special signs to follow. I prefer the late summer to work upland lakes because that is when they are at their prime in beauty and wildlife activity.

Stream Beds. When beachcombing streams and rivers, the object of your search usually is gem materials: agates, jasper, and jade. Although the techniques for streams are similar to those for ocean beaches, you will be in the water more often. Most people stream-comb in water less than two feet deep for three basic reasons: (1) deeper water makes for discomfort in walking; (2) the light refraction in deeper water plays too many tricks on the eyes; and (3) stones can be picked up by hand without getting all wet.

Some seasons are better for stream beachcombing than others. The winter months usually are too cold. In spring, streams and rivers often are roiled up and running full; if they are not, they can become so at any moment—and thus can be dangerous. The best time is late July and August. The levels of the streams are much lower and thus it is easier to look for rocks; but even in the summertime, it is best to comb streams in hip boots and thermal socks.

When going streamcombing, it is helpful to bring along a small steel rod to use as a walking stick and as a pry bar. Often large stones must be moved to get at the smaller ones. A friend of mine used a half-inch solid metal rod about five feet long; it makes a good walking staff and will not float away.

Another friend of mine, Orval Kalkoske, has built a novel viewing tube for looking at the rocky bottom of stream beds for gem materials. In a fast-moving stream the ripples on the surface of the stream make it extremely difficult to see anything beneath the surface of the water. With a tube, you can see everything on the bottom as if the water were standing still on a clear day. On the Teanaway River in Washington, Orval has used his tube to find jade and jade nodules.

To build such a tube, simply take a piece of black plastic pipe about five inches in diameter and eighteen inches in length—or even longer if you don't want to bend too much—cap both ends with pieces of clear plastic. Orval has fixed a pistol grip handle on his tube in order to maneuver it readily through the water. To avoid having the tube bounce away in faster water, attach a short line or lanyard to it and clip the free end to your belt.

Techniques for Special Items

Fossils

Occasionally, beachcombers come across fossil areas. Many fossils are found in ocean shore banks that are layered with sand, clay, and gravel. Larger fossils are located in silt rock layers and can be found by splitting rock pieces open along the cleavage planes with a geologist's hammer. Some shell fossils are as small as the head of a pin and thus must be viewed with a loupe or similar instrument. A small trowel is handy to dig away loose material in the exposed layers along a beach cliff.

A friend in Oregon digging along the side of a stream unearthed something pink in color. He kept digging and came up with a substantial piece of pink agate—the limb of a tree. The limb had been burned up by lava, and the resulting void had filled up with pink agate, giving the beachcomber a unique find.

Agates

Rock beachcombers search the beaches for agates and jasper, the oldest gemstone known to man. The agates found along the Pacific coast can be yellow, orange, red, or black, and their beauty is enhanced by the so-called bark around the outside and the way they are polished.

Agate beachcombing is complicated by the fact that the stones are hard to find. The interested beachcomber should become quite familiar with them before starting the search. If you are unsure about how they look, obtain some samples of agate rock in the rough state. Study them closely when you get to the beach area. Throw the samples out on the sand so that you can see how they look in the prevailing light. Do the same in any differing kind of area—for example, in the gravel bed. When you can readily distinguish the stones, pick out similar pieces as you walk along the beach.

Under certain conditions, agates can readily be detected on gravel beaches, especially on sunny days. Agates will light up or glow when the sun's rays go through them. But you must be careful to distinguish between agate and plain quartz. If it is translucent, it is quartz. By experimenting, determine whether you can spot agates more successfully while walking into the sun or while walking with the sun to your back.

Often the surface condition of an agate attracts the beachcomber. In overcast and rainy weather, the beachcomber can rely only on the texture of the agate to make it recognizably different from other beach rocks; consequently beachcombers must be able to recognize agates in *all* conditions. In any event, the brighter the sunlight on the beach, the better the chances are for the average beachcomber to pick up a few agates.

Artifacts

If you are interested in beachcombing for artifacts, the most productive areas are at the mouths of freshwater rivers and streams. Since Indian fishermen and early settlers used to live along many of these streams, these ancient campsites—plus the river banks near the campsites—often yield artifacts. However, the Indians and the settlers continually changed the locations of their campsites, thus posing a problem for the beachcomber—the original campsites may be covered up or eroded away. One solution to this problem is to travel upstream where it is often possible to identify these historical campsites.

Driftwood

The majority of prizewinning driftwood pieces are now being found at such inland sources as mountain lakes and streams rather than on the ocean beach. Driftwood found on the ocean beach often comes from trees that have fallen from a cliff into the sea or that have been carried down a river. Such pieces get broken up and worked over by the surf and tides. A piece of driftwood from a mountain lake beach, on the other hand, has a better chance of survival in its original configuration than any ocean-borne piece of driftwood. Mountain driftwood even seems to weather better, the windblown, sunburned roots from high altitudes generally being more attractive than driftwood soaked in salt water.

Since beachcombed stumps are much sought after by landscape architects and gardeners for garden design accent material, you should not eliminate them from your search. However, most stumps are large and heavy, and transportation from a beach to one's backyard may be a formidable operation. I once helped to haul a water-soaked stump from a beach on Whidbey Island to a truck, and that still stands as a major accomplishment.

Root driftwood materials, which are decorative and often are used in mobiles and collages, can also be gathered inland, but most of it still comes from the ocean beaches near the mouths of large rivers or streams. During flooding seasons, debris of all sorts is carried down the rivers and out to sea. Uprooted trees, limbs and stumps that float down swollen, freshwater rivers will get a short ocean voyage before being deposited on a beach nearby. The wise beachcomber will pay attention to this seasonal occurrence and will add to his collection when the findings are most plentiful.

Metal Detectors

Many beachcombers today are looking for and finding buried treasure below the surface of the beach sand: Spanish doubloons, cans of coins, gold pieces, rare coins, Civil War souvenirs, revolvers, silver and gold nuggets. All of this and more is available when one uses a portable metal detector. The Sunday afternoon beach browser greatly increases the range of his possible beachcombed treasures when he purchases a metal detector. It will weigh about five pounds and cost from $100-$700.

Brands and Prices

There are many metal detectors on the market with a wide range of capability and price. Without attempting to do an all-inclusive list, the following tabulation gives an idea as to brands and prices:

Brand Name	Manufacturer	Approximate Price
"Gold Star 400"	Compass	*
"Gold Star 200"	Compass	*
"Liberty 100"	Compass	*
"Magnum 240"	Compass	*
"Aquanaut 1280-X"	Fisher	$650
"1235-X"	Fisher	$400
"1265-X"	Fisher	$500
"Master Hunter 7"	Garrett	$600-$700
"Freedom 3"	Garrett	$500
"Beach Hunter AT3"	Garrett	$600
"Gold Hunter"	Garrett	$450
"American AM-2"	Garrett	$200
"Sea Hunter XL500 Pulse"	Garrett	$800
"Mark I LTD"	Teknetics	$700
"Bounty Hunter"	Teknetics	$400

"Coinmaster 6000/Di Pro"	White's	$650
"Coinmaster 5900/Di Pro"	White's	$460
"Coinmaster 4900/D"	White's	$300
"Coinmaster 3900/D"	White's	$300
"Liberty Di"	White's	$560
"Liberty II"	White's	$225
"Liberty I"	White's	$100

*Not available

Techniques

There are two basic kinds of metal detectors, the horizontal coil type and the radio-frequency double coil type. The former is by far the most practical and popular for the beachcomber, and it is considerably less expensive. The latter type is used by professional geologists, prospectors, and field engineers.

Practice with your metal detector and get to know its characteristics. This is the first rule for the beginner. The master of a simple, inexpensive instrument will do better than the inexperienced beginner with the best possible detector. It is well to practice at home over a prescribed training course where you have buried several different metal items at different depths. This can also be done inside the house with coins hidden under the living room rug.

Although you may uncover many valuable items using a purely random approach, larger objects (such as the metal fittings on a hundred-foot sailing ship that has been buried) demand a systematic approach. One such technique is what I call the *grid method*. To use this technique, it is first necessary to establish a baseline across the beach. This original line should be scribed from a tree or large rock out toward an island, mountain, or other landmark; in this way, the baseline could be reproduced again at a later date within the accuracy of about six inches. On each side of this baseline, mark squares in the sand from the edge of the beach down to the water line; the size of the squares will depend on the size of the object you wish to find. The beach now resembles a giant checkerboard.

For the purposes of illustration, let us assume that we are searching for a hundred-foot sailing ship. Measuring fifty-foot squares with a fifty-foot carpenters' tape is simple and will detect any possible position of the hundred-foot ship. For a single afternoon of searching, it will probably be best to scribe no more than ten squares on each

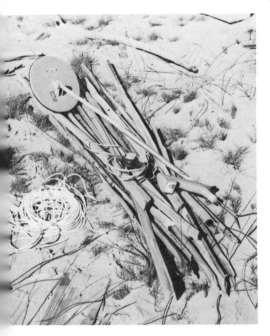

(1) Assemble the necessary equipment: stakes were split from cedar pieces beachcombed at the site; nylon line was knotted at fifty-foot intervals to be used to measure off the squares; and the collapsible metal detector had been carried in a backpack. (2) Establish a baseline and begin marking off fifty-foot squares. (3) Mark squares with large letters that can be read from some distance away. (4) For each square, walk slowly, keeping the antenna plate close to the ground and making a sweep no wider than three feet.

side of the baseline. Then mark each square with a big letter and number, N–1 for the first square north of the baseline, and so on. Then work alternate squares such as the black squares of a checkerboard first—N-1, N-3, N-5, S-2, S-4.

For each square, walk slowly along one side, sweeping the antenna plate of the metal detector evenly across from side to side at a speed of about one foot per second, making a swath about three feet wide, and walking ahead slowly, heel to toe, one foot ahead of the other. The antenna plate should be kept close to the ground during the walk. Continue walking a three-foot wide path in one direction and then back on another, with about sixteen trips per square, not including the stops to mark position coordinates of signal locations. While searching, I have found it a good practice to keep looking out at the horizon and not continuously at the sand, for, after a few hours, this can be tiring on the neck. You should not feel the need to go back once a square has been covered, because this method provides a high probability of coverage on the first pass.

If there is a rise in the tone and a swing of the needle on the meter, stop and determine the center of the signal in fore, aft, and lateral directions; then scribe it on the sand with a stick. Then record the signal location as scribed in a notebook copy of the grid.

Personally, even after getting a strong signal, I prefer to keep going and get as many squares searched as possible. Only after I have marked every signal location in my notebook do I start the digging. Of course the tide of a particular day may dictate where and how much of the beach you can search. After the tide has worked it over, it is virtually impossible to locate any spot on the beach.

Sometimes it may be desirable to extend a search through grass and into a wooded area. Because the antenna plate has to be kept fairly close to the ground, any tough high grass will present a real problem. In the woods I have found the going exceedingly slow, even where the ground is free of brush, because of the general unevenness of the terrain. The better places to work are around tree trunks, yet if a signal comes from the roots, the digging is almost impossible. Unless you are following a well-defined, long-established trail through the woods where metal objects might be lost, the results will be poor.

However, circumstances may lead you to conduct the search in spite of the hazards. We once searched an island that was completely forested because it was known to have been the summer location of about one thousand Indians one hundred years earlier. In the intervening period, good-sized trees had grown up across and through former building sites.

Advantages and Limitations of Metal Detectors

To discover a particular metal item of historical value, one that adds to the knowledge of an area or helps to solve a mystery, is a rare accomplishment and one that is possible using a metal detector. To find the personal possession of an Indian, a hunter, or habitué of the frontier by means of a metal detector is also an achievement of merit. To retrieve a lost wedding ring, an item of great sentimental value, from a swimming beach is to be a good neighbor and perhaps would bring one a monetary reward. This new method that enables anyone to find something previously invisible provides excitement, challenge, and fun to beachcombing. Many metal detectors are sold on the basis of advertisements about stories of buried treasures that have been found. Photographs and testimonials of these findings speak for themselves.

However, the limitations of the metal detector must be understood. Both the working principle and the extent of its application should be known. When the instrument is turned on and tuned properly, an electrical field is excited below the antenna plate. When this field is interrupted by a metal object, a rise in tone will be heard in the earphones and the meter needle will swing. The detection field varies with the type of soil and the amount of moisture in the soil. Even the metallic content of the soil greatly affects the results. I once tried to comb a beach that had bits of iron ore distributed throughout the sand, making the search impossible. Everywhere I went, there was a constant howl and the meter needle constantly registered all the way over.

The likelihood is good of detecting a two-inch-square piece of metal at a two-foot depth, assuming experience on the part of the operator. The probability is similar to that of finding a quarter thrown a few yards ahead of your feet while standing on the front lawn at night and looking for it with a flashlight.

In general, the schedule of a typical metal detector performance is approximately as listed here:

Size of Metal Piece	Maximum Depth for Detection (in average soil conditions)
4 square inches	14 inches
½ square foot	42 inches
1 square foot	6 feet
4 square feet	10 feet

Notice that bigger items at deeper depths will give a signal as strong as smaller items at smaller depths.

The average metal detector will react to metal objects beneath the surface of the sand as small as coins and as large as locomotives. There are a wide variety of things that can be found. On beaches where people congregate to swim, sunbathe, and picnic, many things are lost in the sand that are readily detected—coins, watches, rings, keys, brooches, buttons, hair clips, buckles, cosmetic items, casual jewelry, cigarette lighters, glasses, pocket knives, pencils, and picnic silverware. Generally speaking, these articles are usually picked up in a short period of time thanks to the electronically wired squadron of modern beachcombers. These items are usually recovered in good shape because the metals used in personal effects, such as gold, silver, stainless steel, and copper, all tend to resist rapid corrosion. Another group of articles, not lost but rather discarded and of little value, also are announced by the metal detector. This includes bottle caps, beer cans, aluminum can pull tabs, and packages containing foil.

On beaches that are less frequented by the sunbather, swimmer, or picnicker, most metal articles detected are not personal effects but more general building items such as bolts, driftpins, nails, paint cans, cables, angle irons, chains, tools, and wire. Most of those made of iron or steel are extensively corroded when found, sometimes to several times the original size of the article, and thus are too far gone for further use. For example, rarely have I unearthed a nail that could be used again even for the simplest purpose. I have been able to salvage cadmium-plated spikes, though, from planks that have recently arrived on the beach.

In areas where a shipwreck is known to have occurred, where an

Indian encampment was located, or where a former gold rush took place, there may be historical artifacts covered over by the sand or dirt that can only be discovered by a metal detector. Occasionally a chance digging will uncover an item, but the methodical electronic search is considerably more productive.

The metal detector is not limited to beach use. Many inland areas such as abandoned ranches, logging camps, and mines provide fertile ground for metal detector searching. Further, in desert areas, small meteorites can be found.

Some detectors can be used under water by skin divers to assist in locating shipwrecks. Older American coins have been picked up at long-established county parks, particularly those that had amusements. Fairgrounds and recreational areas near military posts are also good places to cover with a metal detector.

Digging and Sifting

After something has been detected and its location has been marked on the sand, the digging begins. There are several digging tools and sifting screens to make this part of the operation easier.

For the actual digging, be prepared to go several feet deep, although small objects are often located near the surface. I prefer to approach this problem as if I were digging post holes. I like to use a long-handled shovel, which is ideal for holes in the sand down to about three feet. Beyond that depth there are major excavation problems. Some people prefer a short-handled shovel like a spade, but when the hole gets deep, a bigger hole is required to establish a footing. In sand or wet ground, the sides of the hole will fall in, especially if the water table is close to the surface. Thus on a flat, wet, sandy beach it is helpful to have a piece of ten-inch diameter stovepipe about three feet long to push down in order to control cave-in and to concentrate the digging on the scribed location. This pipe acts as a temporary caisson, and with handles attached at one end, it is readily pushed in or taken out. A trowel or small hand shovel, such as a coal or flour scoop, is then needed to dig out the sand within the caisson.

The next step is the sifting. It is best to empty each shovelful of sand onto portable sifting trays, against a leaning screen frame, or into a bucket that has a screen bottom. This will catch such small

Sifting trays designed to nest together conserve space in a backpack.

items as coins that could go unseen if pitched into the tailings. Because of their general utility and compact stowage in a backpack, I like to use half-inch mesh portable sifting trays that fit within one another. Some people like to use a shovel or hand scoop that has a quarter-inch mesh screen built into the bottom so that the sifting can be done in conjunction with the digging. I prefer to work as a part of a two-person team, with one person digging and the other sifting. It is surprising how many dividends, like shells and agates, show up in the sifting.

Tidal Beachcombing

In quiet and protected ocean waters, in and just beyond the tidal areas, there are all sorts of things to beachcomb under the water's surface. Good picking is to be had at harbors, piers, ferry landings, boat marinas, and other places where people congregate. Ferry slips are good places to find bottles and other man-made items because of the continuous washing and scrubbing action of the ferry propellors that changes the bottom. Starfish congregate on the piling and also dig up items from the sand.

When diving the first twenty-five feet, you will find a wide variety of marine organisms, shellfish, and starfish. Beyond that depth a sandy bottom is usually encountered. Here there is a lesser amount of marine growth, so it is easier to locate unusual bottom items. At deeper levels visibility becomes a major problem.

A friend once found a wooden rocking chair at 125 feet, but he stated that in his judgment it was not enough of an antique to salvage. He found much fishing gear that was snagged on the bottom— flashers, plugs, spoons, to name a few items used by salmon fishermen. On another occasion he found an aluminum Danforth anchor that was in excellent shape. Anchors, unlike rocking chairs, do not seem to deteriorate in salt water.

However, these are only a few of the items that you can recover. Sunken hulls are found at almost any depth and can yield some interesting finds. Many divers go after old bottles, a diving fad in recent years. However, it is not necessary to be a diver to find old bottles in tidal waters. Filled or partially filled bottles will roll along the bottom with the currents and will wash up in tidal areas. Near our cabin at Clinton Beach on Whidbey Island, Washington, I once beachcombed quite a rare bottle 150 yards offshore while walking in over the tidal sand flats after anchoring my dinghy at low tide. Bottles will show up every once in a while on these broad sand tidal lands, but they will show almost daily at the high tide level.

Skin Diving and Scuba Diving

Skin diving can be done with or without a wet suit depending on the temperature of the water. A wet suit is standard equipment in Oregon and Washington, while one is rarely seen in Hawaii. The next items of required equipment are: fins, mask, snorkle, and gloves to protect your hands from coral or fish that might sting. A knife is also carried for prying items off rocks or for cutting away the kelp should you become entangled.

For scuba diving (scuba stands for "Self-Contained Underwater Breathing Apparatus"), all of the above items are used plus air tanks, regulator, weight belt to counter tank buoyance, wristwatch for checking air supply, and compass for underwater course control. After some class instruction and training in operational and emergency procedures, the underwater beachcomber is ready to go.

In protected Pacific Ocean waters there are many interesting items to be seen in water less than fifty feet deep. The beautiful underwater plant life is seen down to the twenty-five foot level below low tide line, but beyond that the scenery gets progressively barren. On a sunny day, depending on the condition of the water, there is still some visibility at 120 feet with a circle of vision about twelve feet in diameter. If the sky is overcast, the visibility is cut down considerably.

A mesh bag that will attach onto a belt is an item of special equipment to be used for retrieving items from the ocean floor. Shells and other items are easily carried this way. If something is found that is too heavy for lifting, a special line that has a bobber is attached to the object. After attaching the line, the bobber goes to the surface, and whatever is to be retrieved can be done later by boat.

When searching the bottom, the man-made items often appear as portions of straight lines. A crab pot partially buried on the ocean floor shows as a triangle, an anchor chain appears as a long straight line, a concrete anchor block shows as a square. Once again, it is the alert beachcomber who makes the best finds, but only one who has been properly trained in use of this equipment.

4
Beachcombing Areas—A Detailed Analysis

There are plenty of places to go beachcombing all over the United States. However, I am convinced that the northern Pacific Ocean offers the best opportunities with the southern Atlantic Ocean running a remote second. Perhaps Pacific beachcombing is more profitable because the ocean is the biggest and is bounded by peoples of several different cultures. Certainly the North Pacific Rim circulation pattern is the largest on the globe.

This pattern of course has no starting point; it goes southward along the coast of California, then westward along the tenth parallel below Hawaii to the Philippines, where it turns northeast past Japan, then east to the Pacific Northwest, and south toward California again. The complete circuit on the globe looks like a giant racetrack about eight thousand miles in one direction and three thousand miles in the other. The sharper corners are at the Philippines and off Vancouver Island.

The Japanese Kuroshio Current portion of this large pattern flowing past Japan to the Pacific Northwest is a powerful ocean force, the equivalent of a thousand Mississippi Rivers. At the Vancouver Island turn, the Pacific Current sends an offshoot north and westward toward the Aleutian Chain to form a secondary loop. At this

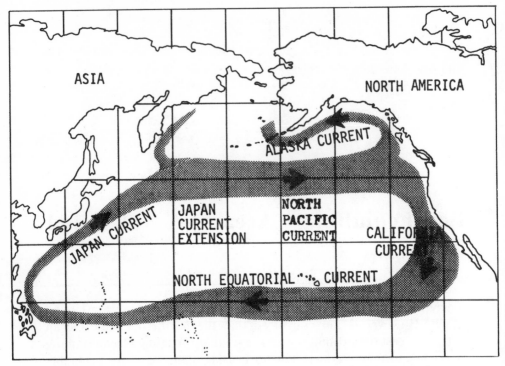

Map 1. The Japan Current

cleavage are the confluences of the Straits of Juan de Fuca and the Columbia River. Combined with storms from Alaska that whiplash our coast, a complex situation is created that may result in one or more maelstroms. At times all this sends ocean-borne flotsam onto our Pacific western shores by sheer centrifugal force.

Bordering the North Pacific Rim are endless ocean beaches— many with rock bluffs that rise for hundreds of feet; others consist of narrow gravel shores, while the most sought after are flat and sandy. For purposes of ready beachcombing classification, I have chosen to divide this 15,000-mile geographic perimeter, all of which is located north of the equator and encompasses about one-eighth of the earth's surface, into twelve separate regions. The beachcomber may choose any one of these regions for his tidal travels and have beach miles to search the rest of his days. I have yet to meet any beachcomber who has completely beachcombed any one of these individual regions.

The regions are: Baja, California, Oregon, Washington, British Columbia, southeastern Alaska, glacial shore Alaska, Alaskan Peninsula, Hawaiian Islands, Marshall Islands, Caroline Islands, and the Marianas Islands. These regions are listed in the following table with information of immediate interest to the prospective beach-comber:

Region	*Estimated Coast Miles*	*Access to Region*	*Population Density*	*Beach-combing Prospects*
Baja	800	All-terrain car	Low	Fair
California	900	Car	High	Fair
Oregon	350	Car	High	Good
Washington	150	Car	Medium	Good
British Columbia	1,000	Car-air-boat	Low	Good
Southeastern Alaska	400	Air-boat	Low	Good
Glacial Shore Alaska	600	Air-boat	Low	Good
Alaskan Peninsula	1,000	Air-boat	Low	Good
Hawaiian Islands	600	Air-boat-car	High	Fair
Marshall Islands	600	Air-boat	Low	Good
Caroline Islands	800	Air-boat	Low	Good
Marianas Islands	400	Air-boat	Low	Good

It is readily seen that even when North Pacific Rim beaches are divided into these general regions there are still hundreds of miles in each region. Many of these Pacific Ocean regions are not readily accessible, and where the interfacing population density is lower, the beachcombing prospects get better. On the other hand, regions of our western Pacific coast such as Baja, California, Oregon, and Washington have some beaches that are easily reached by car; consequently most any resident of the continental United States may enjoy the pleasures of Pacific Ocean beachcombing—if he or she has a mind to.

Baja

Baja California is the Mexican peninsula some 800 miles long and 75 miles wide that extends south of San Diego, California, and is parallel to Mexico's mainland western coast. Baja is exposed to the Pacific Ocean on the west coast and the Sea of Cortez on the east. One may drive the newly paved road for the full length, but much of this peninsula is desert, so there are few towns, gas stations, or residents. There are numerous private campgrounds near the more populated cities and towns that are accommodating the rise in tourist travel.

Pacific Ocean beaches are reasonably accessible for the first 200 miles from Tijuana to El Rosario, but beyond that point, any contact with the western Baja beaches involves an expedition across desert country. Thus one must prepare for the limitations encountered, including emergencies.

Regulations

When entering Baja from the United States, plan on obtaining the required tourist cards, car insurance, and meeting customs regulations on cameras. Before entering Baja, be sure to register all trademarked or foreign-made articles of value at the United States Customs Station. Car permits and health certificates for pets are also required. When returning, $100 worth of Mexican goods can be brought in duty free.

Baja's beaches are public, but almost all of its Pacific Ocean coastal beaches are not readily accessible because of the absence of beach approach roads.

Special Conditions

Baja is not without its dangers. When gathering wood for campfires, watch out for rattlesnakes and scorpions. Some varieties of cacti will jab through leather soles and into automobile tires. Recently a motorcycle racer missed a dirt road turn and drove on until he ran out of gas—and luck—to become a vital statistic. A light airplane was also forced down into a central uninhabited region to add its two pilots to the statistics. Boaters know of Baja's west coast dangers because of the dearth of protected anchorages. Occasionally a cruiser comes to grief when caught in sudden bad weather, and the fate of its occupants becomes headlines. Dangers on the beach are less fatal but

Map 2. Baja coastline

well known—the unannounced *tsunami*, destructive ocean waves, on one side and the unpardoning desert on the other.

Special Equipment

To reach Baja's better beachcombing Pacific beaches in its central portion, it will require a 75-mile drive, one way, from the main road on an unmarked trail across the Vizcaino Desert and rough mountain country. The special equipment required for this trek is principally a four-wheel drive vehicle capable of carrying all the fuel, water, food, camping gear, and creature comforts for the intended duration of the beach visit. Emergency equipment must include a good automobile jack, complete tool kit, tow rope, two spare tires, tire removal tools, spark plug tire inflator, and battery jumper cables. The spare parts recommended are: spare fuel pump, coil, points, condenser, fan belts, extra engine oil, spark plugs, wiring, hoses and clamps, fuses, extra set of keys, a chamois for straining local gasoline. At the beaches, be prepared for hot bright days and cold foggy nights in a locale with an annual rainfall of one to three inches. No special beachcombing equipment as such is required.

Relative Value

The relative value of central western Baja as a beachcombing area is exceedingly high. Due to its remoteness and the problems to be overcome in order to set foot on these beaches, the opportunities for prime beachcombing are excellent. If I were to choose four of the best Pacific Ocean beach areas, Baja's central western coast would be one.

Prime Areas

Although San Quintin in the northern portion of Baja is quite productive, the central area has its fabulous Malarrimo Beach. Bordering Vizcaino Bay, it runs east and west curving in a barely perceptible graceful arc for eighteen miles. At the western end is a rocky headland; at the eastern end is Scammon's Lagoon, well known as a mating place for the gray whale. Malarrimo is especially productive since Vizcaino Bay, with its adjoining protrusion of land into the Pacific, acts as a storage or catch basin. The advantage of this topog-

Malarrimo Beach is perhaps the most productive beach in Baja, as this photo indicates (Mike McMahan Photo)

raphy is strengthened by the coastwise southbound California Current, which is forced westerly in this region before proceeding south or southwesterly. The prevailing winds are northerly in this region from November to June, with wind speeds ten to forty knots—ideal conditions for current-borne debris to be deposited on adjacent downwind shores. However, with a shallow dangerous shore on one side, moving sand dunes on the desert side, and no access at either end, this beach is out of reach for all but the determined adventure-bound beachcomber.

As to what you will find, the first signs of beach drift appear fully fifteen miles inland—massive redwood logs and stumps, left from some devastating tsunami wave of years past. The beach proper may have such things as life jackets, Japanese glass fishing floats, airplane wreckage, steamer deck chairs, ships' hatch covers, tin cans of emergency rations and other foods, and torpedoes—all of which were reported on a single trip by author Mike McMahan. He located pieces from ancient wooden sailing ships, some that might well have been from the legendary Manila Galleon fleet. Bottles, life rings, rope, oars, boxes with oriental markings, sandals, brooms, basketballs, and many unidentified items could be added to the list.

Non-beach Beachcombing

As for non-beach beachcombing, Baja provides: petroglyphs to be found and admired; numerous scenes, views, or backdrops for the photographer to capture; and practical philosophy as related by its natives.

California

Like everything else in California, its Pacific coast is lengthy, inconsistent, and incomprehensible. Its sprawling 900 plus miles of steep rock cliffs with gravel or sand beaches is the western boundary for some 27 million people. This relatively narrow beach strip along the Pacific, the world's greatest natural barrier, provides a shoreline along which California's population explosion and expansion are readily experienced. Here recreational pursuits flourish. Many beaches daily available to Golden State residents are continuously crisscrossed with myriads of footprints upon footprints. Only when the higher tides

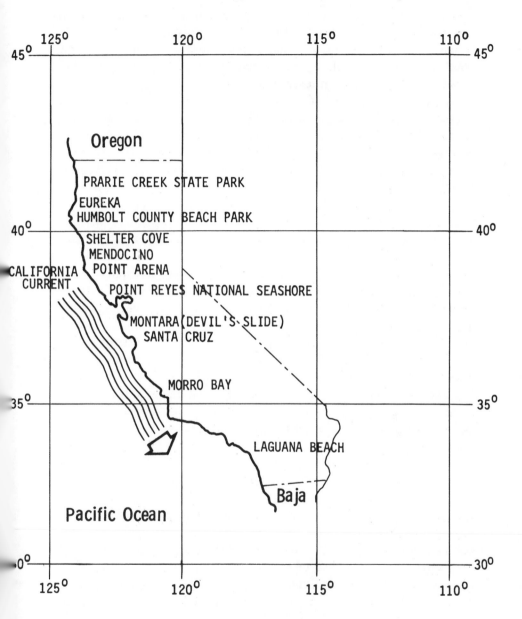

Map 3. California coastline

flatten out the sands do these footprints disappear. This foot traffic on California's central and southern beaches has given birth to a special beachcombing art. In these more populated areas, some beachcombers probe the sands with electronic metal detectors to find money, jewelry, and other lost valuables.

California has over 100 public coastal state parks, beaches, recreational areas, reserves, campgrounds, and historic parks—about one every eight miles. By contrast, private beaches are the luxury afforded to owners of extensive land holdings. California's northern beach areas are generally less accessible and have fewer nearby cities to increase the westward tilt.

Regulations

Most coastal cities have ordinances covering use of beaches within their corporate limits. State parks, beaches, etc., are protected by state law. Military reservations are generally off limits to the beachcomber. Coastal federal lands like the Los Padros National Forest and Point Reyes National Seashore have their own regulations that are posted.

Because the state's tidal pools were being overstudied by busloads of school children, the Fish and Game Commission has adopted regulations to prevent abuse and waste of this resource. These regulations outlaw general collection of tidal invertebrates in tide pools and other areas between the high tide mark and 1,000 feet beyond the low tide mark without a written permit from the Department of Fish and Game. The exceptions are: first, in state and national parks, state beaches and reserves, visitors may take abalones, chiones, clams, cockles, crabs, lobsters, scallops, and sea urchins; and second, in all other areas, except within marine life refuges and other closed areas, persons may take abalones, chiones, clams, cockles, crabs, limpets, lobsters, mussels, sand dollars, octopi, shrimp, scallops, sea urchins, and squid. A current California sport fishing license is necessary to take the invertebrates listed, and their take is restricted by seasonal, bag, and size limits.

Beachcombing restrictions are often a matter of private ownership of the adjacent lands. Some beaches are available only through private land, thus tolls or fees are collected at some of these for the privilege of using approach roads. Some private beach areas are barricaded or have posted warnings at the property lines.

There is one final restriction that all must abide by: when one approaches the California border, one must be prepared for a search by the state fruit inspectors.

Special Conditions

The dangerous parts of this coastline are the steep bluffs and banks that line much of the coast. Such a place is Devil's Slide near Montara. Most of these have posted warnings and some are fenced. Otherwise, the sections that have broad flat sandy beaches are generally quite safe for hiking and picnicking.

A second danger that may be present is in rock-bound shores below bluffs where one might be caught by a sneaker ocean wave and be lost in the undertow.

Special Equipment

California beachcombing is straightforward, particularly where the beach is wide enough to provide some ocean flotsam. Because of mild coastal weather conditions, no special equipment is required beyond a rucksack to carry your treasure.

Relative Value

As a beachcombing region, the lengthy California coastline with all its variety of cliffs and access problems qualifies as an average territory. The high population density and the popularity of beach recreational activities also make it a highly competitive beachcombing region. Its southern beaches are considered to be less productive, its central beaches fair, and its northern beaches good. California's size tends to monopolize our western Pacific coastline. If pure beachcombing is one's prime interest, then stick to the northern third of the coastline; if scenic beauty is the main objective, then go to the middle third; but if swimming, sandy beaches, and people are your purpose, then hike the southern third.

Prime Areas

Regarding some of the better areas in the southern region, try

Laguna Beach, Morro Bay, and Santa Cruz. In the central region, visit the Point Reyes National Seashore, Point Arena, and Mendocino. For the northern region, hike the Shelter Cove to the Eureka area, Humbolt County Beach Park, and Gold Beach in Prairie Creek State Park for starters. All of these places are readily accessible from coastal Highway 1.

Non-beach Beachcombing

Considerable non-beach beachcombing is done with metal detectors at inland ghost towns, abandoned mining and logging areas, and former places of habitation. Many of the smaller and upper level river beds are also worked for their precious stones and metals.

In state parks, flowers, rocks, plants, animals, and other natural features of park areas are protected by state law and may not be disturbed or collected. Driftwood, however, is not considered a natural part of the environment and its collection may be allowed in lakes and reservoirs within state parks. Many coastal and beach parks permit the collecting of driftwood. Collectors should inquire at the park office for regulations in effect.

Oregon

Oregon has about 350 miles of beautiful coastline, and fully ninety percent of this total is flat and sandy. Occasionally a rocky headland will jut out, but soon enough there is another fine walkable beach. Because of the many state-protected beaches, Oregon is a beachcomber's heaven.

The charms of the Oregon coast are many. These beaches are directly accessible, and they have all-year-around recreational use thanks to the stabilizing climatic effect of the offshore Pacific Ocean Current. The fascination of sand dunes, rocky cliffs, and wide flat beaches with snow-capped mountains for a backdrop is readily acclaimed by all who travel there. The many and ever-changing moods of the Pacific Ocean are readily experienced on this coast.

The Oregon beaches are well known for their resident beachcombers who patrol on a twenty-four hour basis. Nothing that rolls in from the surf on an Oregon beach will remain undiscovered very long. It will be picked up within hours by one of this beach fraternity. Not

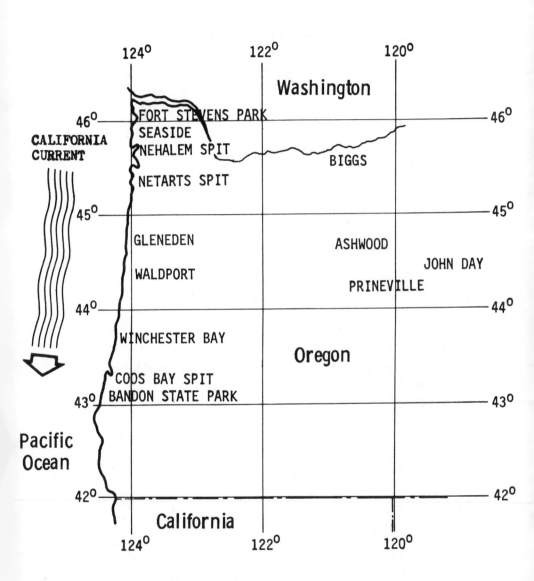

Map 4. Oregon coastline

very much gets past this crowd. A newcomer will have to be out there early in the morning to pick up his share.

Part of the reason for the active participation and interest in beach recreation pursuits is the relatively high number of small towns along the Oregon coast. When driving the coastal route, one passes through one small town after another. Furthermore, there are large cities within a few hours drive of the beach; many an Oregon resident will enjoy his Pacific Ocean on a Sunday afternoon for someone's saying, "Let's go to the coast."

Regulations

Virtually all the coastal beach of Oregon is public domain. Very few private or government areas restrict the prowlings of foot-bound beachcombers. Driving on the beaches here is covered by state statute and is enforced by the State Highway Division, and the Highway Commission's official *Oregon Highway Map* clearly denotes the degree of restriction that relates to vehicle use on the beaches for the entire coast. These restrictions vary continuously along the coast depending on the specific beach and its proximity to nearby population centers.

The degree of restriction varies all the way from "Vehicles Allowed" to "Vehicles Prohibited." The estimated miles for each category of restrictions for the total Oregon coastline is listed here:

Vehicles Allowed	145 miles	(42%)
Vehicles Allowed, May 1 to Sept. 30,		
Sunrise to Sunset	2 miles	(1%)
Vehicles Allowed, Oct. 1 to April 30,		
7:00 A.M. to 12:00 Noon	2 miles	(1%)
Vehicles Prohibited, May 1 to		
Sept. 15, Noon to Midnight	4 miles	(2%)
Vehicles Prohibited, May 1 to		
Sept. 30	40 miles	(11%)
Vehicles Prohibited	151 miles	(43%)

In general, beach driving prohibitions have been established at beach areas where all-year-around beach use is high, meaning that the population density near that beach is high. Thus, prime recreational beach areas are protected throughout the year. Other areas are vehicle-prohibited only during the summer months when the seasonal use is high. Some beach areas that are not subject to high recreational use have all-year-around vehicle usage. Study of the Highway Commission map also indicates that there was consideration given to special use areas. For example, dune vehicle use was retained at the Oregon Dunes National Recreational Area.

Chapter 390 of the current Oregon Revised Statutes states: "It is the public policy of the State of Oregon to forever preserve and maintain the sovereignty of the state heretofore legally existing over the ocean shore . . . so that the public may have the free and uninterrupted use thereof." Also the Legislative Assembly further declares "that it is in the public interest to do whatsoever necessary to preserve and protect scenic and recreational use of Oregon's ocean shore." There in quite positive language is what the people of the State of Oregon, through their legislative process, have declared relative to access and use of its beaches.

Chapter 390 also legalizes activities of the beachcomber under the special permit section. That statute states that "no sand, rock, mineral, marine growth or other natural product of the ocean shore, other than fish or wildlife, agates or souvenirs, shall be taken from the state recreational areas."

Oregon is one of the few states that has a treasure-trove provision, which states in part: "The State Highway Commission may prescribe rules and issue permits governing the exploration for, and removal of, treasure-trove, semiprecious stones, petrified wood, and archaeological and paleontological objects from the recreational areas. . . ." Should a beachcomber find the remains of a Spanish Manila Galleon, a permit could be obtained to salvage its cargo. However twenty-five percent of its cargo value must be turned over to the Commission.

The Oregon coast contains about twenty miles of federal beach land of the Siuslaw National Forest. There are also over seventy state, federal, and county parks, waysides, and recreational areas along this coast—an average of about one every five miles.

Special Conditions

Because of the high percentage of its wide sandy beaches, Oregon has few special conditions. Beach visitors must be alerted to two possible dangers. First is the unannounced sneaker wave. This is usually a single wave that is considerably higher than the rest of the wave pattern, and when it comes in on shore, it will tumble along anything in its path up to or behind the main tide line. Automobiles driving a beach at night have been carried toward the high tide line by sneaker waves. Sneaker waves have been known to capsize fishing boats at sea. They usually come without warning; however, when approaching a flat beach, there may be a momentary pronounced recession of the undertow before striking. Technically these are junior-grade versions of tsunami, great sea waves produced by underwater earth movement or volcanic eruption. On any Pacific Ocean flat coastal area like Oregon, when beachcombing in low tidal gravel areas for agates, always face the ocean side and keep a weather eye to sea. If there is a major change in the roar of the surf, run as fast as you can for high ground.

The second danger to watch for on a beach heavy with driftwood are the eighty-foot-long boom logs left in a random crisscross fashion after being refloated during high tides. These six-ton logs may start rolling off one another at the slightest push—thus, they are deadly.

Special Equipment

For Oregon beaches, there is no special equipment required for the average beachcomber hike, other than to have clothing matched for the weather. A rucksack is convenient to carry the larger items that you want to bring home, such as pieces of oriental woods, teredo wood, driftwood, bottles, and fishing floats.

Relative Value

As a beachcombing territory, Oregon is one of the better regions. Its Pacific coastline provides a natural depository for debris that is driven in by coastal storms from the ocean currents. The Oregon coast has long been an active beachcombing area. Thus many Oregonians know about this recreational pastime and actively pursue

Beachcomber finds broken sign and bucket in driftwood strewn along Pacific Ocean coast at *Salishan* Beach, Oregon. (Bert Webber Photo)

Beachcomber examines a piece of driftwood from the wide array of beach drift on Nehalem Spit, Oregon.

it. What Oregon beachcombers display at coast beach festivals is a representative and accurate account of what is drifting by in the slowly moving offshore California Current. In other words, if it is floating in the Pacific, Oregon beachcombers sooner or later will find it on their beaches and show it at their festivals.

Prime Areas

It is hard to think of an individual beach along the Oregon coast that is not a producing area. The few rock bluff headlands usually have no beaches; however, much of the Oregon coast contains driftwood at the high tide line—always a good sign for beachcombing. I recommend such places as Bandon State Park, Coos Bay Spit, Winchester Bay, Waldport, Gleneden, Netarts Spit, Nehalem Spit, and Fort Stevens Park. This in no way names all the good places.

As to what you will find here, imagine a giant cornucopia with an endless amount of oriental flotsam spilling out at your feet. This harvest will be stretched out along the tide lines, but I can assure you, you will have company while you are doing the searching. One item that is unique to the Oregon coast is the Spanish Manila Galleon beeswax that is still being found occasionally near Nehalem. Because of this, Nehalem Spit is the second on my list of four best beachcombing spots around the North Pacific Rim.

Non-beach Beachcombing

There is considerable non-saltwater beachcombing in Oregon. Rockhounds do a lot of river bank combing throughout the state. Some eastern and central areas are known worldwide for their geodes, agates, and other semiprecious stones. Many a group has worked the regions near Prineville, Biggs, Ashwood, and John Day. Upper areas are searched by taxidermists for branch pedestal mounts for birds and animals.

Washington

Washington has about 150 miles of Pacific Ocean waterfront. In addition, there are several times that amount of inland saltwater frontage when considering Juan de Fuca Strait, Admiralty Inlet, Puget Sound, Whidbey Island, the San Juan Islands, Grays Harbor, and

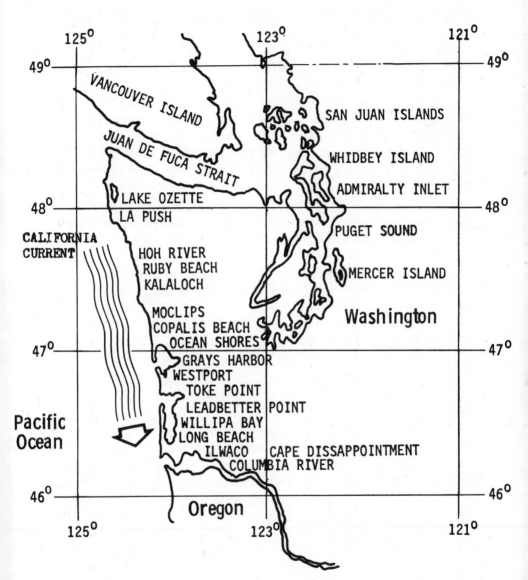

Map 5. Washington coastline

Willapa Bay. Even though these inland areas are only secondarily affected by ocean and coastal currents, these beaches are also good for beachcombing local drift items. For example, out on the Pacific coast one finds oriental flotsam, at the Straits one finds marine gear, and in Puget Sound one finds dimension lumber and log bark.

The southern half of Washington's Pacific coastal beaches are flat, sandy, and driftwood-laden, which is a continuation of the pattern established by northern Oregon beaches. Forming the southern boundary of Washington State, the Columbia River, four miles wide at its mouth, well may have established the nature of these beaches. The 20-mile-long peninsula just north of the Columbia River from Ilwaco to Leadbetter Point appears to be the result of thousands of years of tidal coastwise flow of Columbia River deposits. About 20 miles north beyond Willapa Bay are two more spits guarding Grays Harbor. All of these coastal spit areas have extremely flat beaches with a slope of about 1/100 (a rise of one foot for every 100 feet of distance). Most of these beaches are readily available by car, and many are drivable.

The northern half of Washington coastal beaches are generally rock bluffs lined with narrow beaches punctuated with boulders of all sizes, as well as rocks and gravel. The slopes of these beaches average about 1/10, meaning that less drift is apt to accumulate here.

Regulations

The State of Washington Department of Natural Resources is responsible for the management and administration of a major portion of the state-owned beds and shores of navigable waters. They have no objection to recreational beachcombing on publicly owned lands, so long as no merchantable materials are removed. In speaking of merchantable materials, they mean timber, sand, gravel, etc.

In Puget Sound, the state has disposed of approximately sixty percent of the tidelands, the area lying between the line of mean high tide and the line of extreme low tide. Thus a beachcomber in Puget Sound will need to determine whether his activity is on state-owned land or on privately owned property; if he is on the latter, he is trespassing.

Along the Pacific Ocean, the Washington State Seashore Conservation Area has been established as a means of controlling lands between the line of ordinarily high tide and the line of extremely low tide, as well as all state-owned nontrust accreted lands along the ocean. Indian reservations are excluded. This means that almost all of the Pacific Ocean tidelands in the State of Washington are in the public domain and that these coastal beaches are preserved for public recreation.

Recreational use is the province of the Washington State Parks and Recreation Commission. This commission has established driving regulations to protect the beach and its visitors. A "drivable beach" is defined as the area of firm, wet sand upland from the clam beds over which the tide ebbs and flows daily. This area is considered hard enough to support the weight of an ordinary passenger vehicle and provide traction for the tires. The dry sand area is everything upland from the water line, except for this strip of firm, wet sand that is designated as drivable beach. Parking is permitted only in the landward 100 feet of the drivable beach. The regulations covering motor vehicles also apply to horses.

Firewood cutting is permitted on weekdays only on certain beaches and with permission of the nearest park ranger. Gathering of specimens of driftwood, rocks, and shells on ocean beaches is permissible anytime, as long as the use of power tools is not involved.

The commission has also protected such inedible species as starfish, sea urchins, sand dollars, and sea anemones found on state park beaches. Removal of any sea life is prohibited, except those edible varieties defined and regulated by the State Department of Fisheries.

Within the northern half of Washington's Pacific coast is the 45-mile Olympic National Park strip. Regulations here, as in other national parks, prohibit use of motorized vehicles, thus the hiking trails are for hikers and packers. Instructions covering beach hiking and camping along this ocean park are included in a packet of information given by Park Service Rangers to hikers entering the area. The packet consists of two maps, a trail mileage chart, a tide table for the current two months, and the cover page of general information, which is repeated here:

BEACH HIKING

The last wilderness beach in the contiguous United States is found between Cape Alava and Rialto Beach, LaPush (3rd beach) and the Hoh River. This popular beach offers changing scenic views of ocean, cliffs, headlands and numerous small islands. Beach combing and the perpetual search for Japanese fishing floats add considerable interest to this area.

This is a rugged wild section of coastline and nature calls the shots. One should plan a beach hike with tides in mind. You can't round many of the headlands on an incoming tide, or some, like Taylor Point, at low tide or at night. Never hike alone and always register at a ranger station or registration box at the trailhead.

Trails to the beach are maintained and easy to walk; however, the trails over the headlands are often steep and muddy. Both headland trails and trails that lead to the roads are marked at their beginning with an orange and black disc. Your registration card serves as a fire permit. Fires built against driftwood are dangerous and illegal.

We ask you to accept the responsibility of helping us maintain the integrity of this last wild stretch of beach. Respect it, leave it unimpaired and cleaner than you found it.

Again, along the northern half of the Washington coast are the Quinault, Ozette, and Makah Indian Reservations comprising about 35 miles of beach. These posted areas are now off limits to non-Indians.

Washington has a large number of state parks adjoining salt-water shores. These park lands, as are all privately owned lands, are off limits to beachcombing. State statute prohibits removal of any object from state park land; thus, anything above the high tide line is protected.

Special Conditions

Dangerous conditions along Washington's coast are essentially the same as on the Oregon coast, namely sneaker waves and boom logs left jackstraw fashion after high tides. For beach hikers there are

Beachcomber of Ocean Shores, Washington, displays custom-made beach car he built from a World War II jeep.

a few headlands to cross when the tide is high, so watch for the slippery places. The rainfall along this coast will exceed 100 inches per year, and the Hoh River rain forest with all its moss is well named. In the Olympic National Park beach strip, be on the watch for the occasional bear. If you return to a messed up campsite, a bear has visited you in search for food. It is best to cache your food in a tree away from the campsite.

Special Equipment

For Washington beachcombing, the beachcombing hiker who will visit the Olympic National Park strip will want some equipment for overnight use. The isolated region of the beach, plus the three-mile hike necessary to get into the beach past Lake Ozette, may dictate overnight camping; so, in this area, hikers with backpacks containing camping gear are the norm. This means sleeping bag, tent or tarp, food, cooking gear, and rain clothes are a must for this trek. There are a few shelters along the coastal strip, but availability of these cannot be depended upon. Many beach hikers take the 20-mile beach hike from La Push to Lake Ozette with two overnight stops. For those not prepared for that much hiking, the beachcombing interest dwindles on the second day. If a single twelve-inch Japanese glass fishing float is found, one must make the decision whether to add the ten pounds onto the thirty-five-pound pack for the remaining ten miles, assuming average pack weights and midway point for the float find.

Relative Value

The Washington coast as a Pacific coast beachcombing territory rates good despite its exceedingly low linear mileage, which is the shortest of any of the regions considered. The flat beaches along the southern half catch considerable debris and are readily available by car. The steeper beaches of the northern half are isolated enough to keep out most people except the weekend hikers. Elaine and I have beachcombed the Sand Point coastal area in the Olympic National Park beyond Lake Ozette in a single day. This ten-mile hike was made in comparative ease; however, our beachcombing success was limited to about fifteen pounds of floats, so the return trek proved no problem. Even so, for us it involved one overnight stay at Port Angeles, Washington, with established civilization amenities. We have hiked and camped in the Olympic National Park enough to call it home, and the Lake Ozette coastal beachcombing hike is a favorite.

Other reasons that make Washington a good beachcombing region is its coastal winter storm patterns, its distance from the larger cities, and its proximity to the California Current, which has been sighted as close as five miles offshore. The coastal towns may be crowded in the summertime and on holiday weekends, but the rest of the time there is plenty of solitude and oriental debris to go around.

Prime Areas

One could say that the best areas along the southern half of the Washington coast are from Cape Disappointment to Leadbetter Point, Toke Point to Westport, and Ocean Shores to Ruby Beach. For my limited precious beachcombing hours assigned to the southern Washington coast, I prefer Ocean Park, Copalis, and Iron Springs; but beachcomber friends could do as well at Long Beach, North Cove, and Moclips. For the northern half, there is general agreement for Kalaloch, La Push, and Ozette.

Anywhere on Washington's outer coastal beaches there can be found Japanese glass fishing floats, plastic floats, bottles, fishing gear, teredo wood, agates, jasper, driftwood, pieces of ships, and a wide variety of oriental debris.

"Big Root," a landmark on the beach at Ocean Shores, Washington, appears to be well anchored in the sand about one hundred yards out from the line of vegetation.

Non-beach Beachcombing

Considerable lowland and upland fresh water lake searching goes on. There is much hiking along rivers and streams for a variety of man-made and nature-carved items. Rockhounds search for blue gem agates, geodes, jasper, fossil crabs, and petrified wood in the Cascade Mountains and the central regions of the state. Burls, driftwood, and grasses are also sought.

British Columbia

When the Pacific Ocean collides with the outer coast of British Columbia, it is resisted by a number of islands; beyond these islands is a series of inlets, some measuring 50 miles in length. British Columbia's coast is also guarded by Vancouver Island on the southern third and the Queen Charlotte Islands on the northern third. Thus, one can only arbitrarily estimate that British Columbia has a 1,000-mile coastal shoreline; this distance includes the outside of Vancouver Island plus both sides of the Queen Charlotte Islands and is measured across all inlets. Both sides of the Queen Charlottes are included in this estimate since they are 60 miles offshore; thus, the Alaska Current may affect both sides.

The whole outer coast of British Columbia is unique. Most of it is rocky, but there are isolated beaches that collect Kuroshio drift.

However, accessibility is a problem. Facing the ocean in all this distance is less than 100 miles of coast access road. Vancouver Island, between Ucluelet and Tofino, accounts for 30 miles of this distance. The rest is on the Queen Charlotte Islands at the east and north sides of Graham Island. Consequently, these are the popular areas. Since, for the rest of British Columbia, there is no automobile access, all beachcombing must be done by boat or airplane.

With the difficulties of road access, isolation, ruggedness of the outer coastal area, plus the annual rainfall of 180 inches, it is a small wonder that there are villages on the outer coast. Those that do exist are dependent on fishing, mining, or logging.

There are isolated and intermittent stretches of sandy beaches all along the outer coast of Vancouver Island, the Queen Charlotte Islands, and the short central exposed region of the British Columbia mainland. On the average, these beaches account for no greater than one-fourth of the total coastal mileage, while the other three-fourths remain rockbound ocean frontage.

Regulations

It is comforting to learn that almost all British Columbia beaches are in the public domain. Government land holdings, national or provincial parks, lighthouse sites, and coast rescue stations account for most of the areas that are off limits; Indian reserves, marinas, and oyster leases account for less area but are also off limits. Indian reserves are readily identified on charts and maps of the outer coast and are to be respected. The reserves are often located near river mouths and areas that in the past were close to runs of fish or were readily accessible to clam beds and other food sources.

Special Conditions

Because of the challenging coastal geography, beachcombing is rarely pursued unless in conjunction with some other activity such as fishing. Also, this is not the thing to do all by yourself. Even in the best of weather, the practical considerations of getting to an outer beach by boat, and then anchoring or beaching, is still a recommended two-person operation. Even travel by kayak should be done

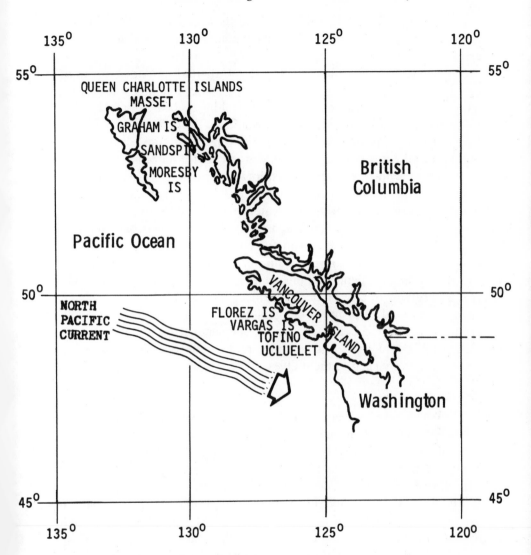

Map 6. British Columbia coastline

with a partner. Travel by outboard into these coastal waters will run the risks of fog, submerged rocks, mechanical failure, and navigation error.

The dangers of beachcombing this Canadian province are ever present, as are the elements of the stormy Pacific. The first category of dangers are those encountered while traveling by boat. For example, to prepare for the 20-mile run by outboard from Tofino to Flores Island on a sunny day, you would still want charts and a compass, blankets and extra clothes, food and water, extra gasoline and tools, two anchors with line, waterproofs, a tarp for emergency shelter, and a signaling device—even though you are in constant sight of land along the way and in protected waters much of the time. Areas exposed to the ocean experience coastal swells, and when bad weather begins to show, it is time to run for cover. The occasional whale or basking shark may also give one an inferior feeling. The open Pacific is a demanding element, and one must abide by its rules for survival. It is unforgiving of any carelessness, incapacity, or neglect.

The second category of dangers are those encountered once you get to your selected beach. These include sneaker waves, heavy surf, precarious boom logs, and slippery rocks. The occasional bear or cougar generally keep to themselves.

Special Equipment

In addition to the equipment mentioned above, the beachcomber will want special equipment such as a rucksack, a jackknife, a small hand shovel, and pliers, in order to be prepared for the unusual. Of greater importance is the need for raingear and warm clothing that will afford adequate protection in a rain-driven storm condition. Boots are best for driftwood hiking and rock climbing; tennis shoes are best when streams are encountered. So take your pick, depending on what the beachcombing task might be that particular day. If it is to be a long hike over a wide variety of terrain I wear boots and carry the tennis shoes in my pack.

Relative Value

British Columbia shores get a high rating as a beachcombing area for four reasons: remoteness, inaccessibility of its beaches, close proximity of the Alaska Current, and low population density. On most British Columbia beaches, items carried in by storm and tide will not be immediately discovered as is the case on California and Oregon shores. Even with the many fishermen who beachcomb for diversion while waiting for favorable weather at some secluded location, there are beaches that get visited only a few times each year. The coastal residents who get into these beaches after the spring storms find a number of fascinating beach drift items.

Typical summer beachcomber finds from Bartlett Island, British Columbia, include piece of Japanese wood dunnage, plastic floats, plastic line, and a fisherman's gaff (above, left). Typical scene on outer Vancouver Island, British Columbia. Although high tides and winds have driven beach logs up into the salal, beachcombing this far up generally is not very productive (above, right).

Prime Areas

To approach some of the better beachcombing areas, it is suggested that you trailer a boat to Tofino on Vancouver Island. Weather permitting, head northwest along the coast to Vargas or Flores Islands to the outer beaches that face the ocean. This will mean anchoring in protected waters and hiking to the outer areas. Numerous day trips like this can be made out of Tofino. The variety of things to be found on these outer beaches after spring storms will run the full gamut from pill bottles to pieces of broken ships—glass fishing floats, marine gear, and oriental flotsam included.

Other accessible beach areas of British Columbia are on the Queen Charlotte Islands. To get there, fly from Vancouver to Sand Spit airport on Moresby Island, take the bus and ferry to Queen Charlotte City, and hire a car for the 80-mile drive to Masset. This brings you to the northern and eastern shores of Graham Island.

For the number three beach on my list of four favorite beaches around the Pacific rim, I choose a spot north of Frederick Island on the isolated west coast of Graham Island. Because of access and prevailing weather conditions in this region of the Queen Charlotte Islands, this area is not readily available; thus the beach drift accumulations are outstanding. A visitor who came by boat found the remains of a seaplane that apparently had been damaged beyond repair during takeoff in extreme weather conditions.

To try for almost any other part of British Columbia, you will have to mount an expedition to get into isolated beaches—all of which are many miles from a motel. Prospectors and geologists employing helicopter charter services in their searchings often run into prime remote beaches in their travels and find many prized items.

Non-beach Beachcombing

Freshwater beachcombing also goes on in British Columbia. The glaciation on Vancouver Island has scattered many rockhound treasures far and wide. There are fossil banks and gold panning to be had in the rivers, and upper lake regions produce driftwood for craftwork projects.

Southeastern Alaska

This 400-mile region between Ketchikan and Cape Spencer provides some excellent beachcombing. There are several rows of islands off the coast in this region, so actual waterline beach miles may be ten times the airline distance of the outer coast. Since much of this mileage is rocky, the sand beaches are well known to the fishermen, hunters, and pilots who frequent this area.

Regulations

Generally speaking there are no restrictions on occasional beachcombing activity. Beachcombing is often a secondary activity to hunting or fishing, and these are regulated by governmental agencies.

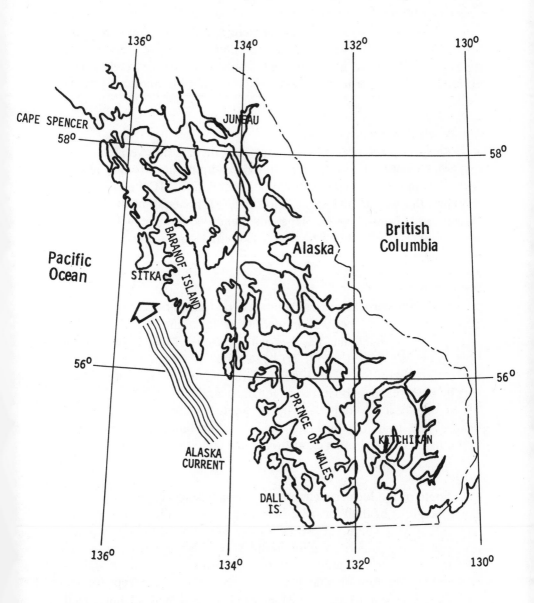

Map 7. Southeastern Alaska coastline

Special Conditions

The dangers of beachcombing here are weather, human error, and predators. All beachcombing is done by boat, airplane, or helicopter. There are no connecting roads, only short stretches near communities; thus, transportation from one island to another is by air or boat.

Special Equipment

Since beachcombing by airplane may involve an overnight stay, the usual creature comforts for outdoor camping are brought along: tent, sleeping bag, cooking equipment, and food. If the trip is by airplane, the weight and cubic allowance of this equipment must be considered. Usually the airplane emergency equipment will include such items as a rifle, extra blankets, clothing, food, water, and a signaling device.

Relative Value

As a beachcombing area, southeastern Alaska ranks high. Beach accessibility is low, population density is low, and the changeable weather fills isolated flat beaches with treasure. Most beaches here have considerable driftwood. To beachcomb this region, one should fly to Ketchikan, Sitka, or Juneau. From there, one can organize a trip by bush plane or boat. Arrangements can be made to be dropped off at one beach and picked up at another. These seldom visited beaches are available by boat, floatplane, or landplane, depending upon the geography, open exposure, beach conditions, and weather.

Prime Areas

Some of the local beachcombing pilots prefer not to disclose the exact locations of their favorite beaches; however, they will not hesitate to take you where you would like to go. Some of the beaches are exclusive to the finders. A pilot friend visits a beach each year to fill his plane with beachcombed trophies; according to his observations no one else sets foot on that beach in between visits—except for the predators. General areas to consider are Prince of Wales Island, Dall Island, and Baranof Island; however, there are hundreds of other specific locations equally as productive. Study of charts for this area is a

This vista, near Cape Addington, is typical of most of southeastern Alaska. Although no floating items can be expected to remain here, the Alaskan beachcomber can enjoy the awesome beauty of the area. (Dick Hamlin Photo)

Pam Hamlin shows beachcombed loot from "Sandpiper" float airplane expedition in southeastern Alaskan shores. Roller float, saki bottles, soy sauce bucket, plastic floats, and gill net glass fishing floats, all from off shore Japanese fishing operations make for a highly successful afternoon of beach searching and hiking. Note the occasional pile of seagrass at the high tide line deposited there by previous tides and storms. (Dick Hamlin Photo)

must. Any number of items can be found in this region, including Japanese glass fishing floats, bottles, ivory, pieces of ships, plus a never-ending list of unusual items that make their way into these waters.

Glacier Shore Alaska

This 600-mile coastline of Alaska extends from Cape Spencer west to Cook Inlet. Glaciers bound much of this part of the coast, but Pacific Ocean drift makes its way onto these exposed shores, especially on the occasional sandspit. The ocean drift is brought to this region by the Alaska Current, which is going west in this part of the Pacific.

Regulations

In this part of Alaska, there are few incorporated communities to regulate beach activities. Government areas are limited to the few isolated Coast Guard stations, lighthouses, navigation stations, and national forests.

Special Conditions

As to the special dangers in this region, there is the sloughing of the glaciers, the floating ice from the glaciers, and earth slides. Once, at Lituya Bay, a side of a mountain gave way, forcing the bay waters up the other side to an elevation of about 1,000 feet, all of which denuded the immediate region of its timber.

Special Equipment

Since most areas have a high surf, most beachcombing here is done by air or from the few logging roads. There is no unique special equipment required here other than what has already been mentioned. The changeable weather determines any travel, and protected moorages are hard to come by. Special attention must be given to tie down aircraft overnight.

Relative Value

As a beachcombing territory, glacier shore Alaska ranks high. Most of this region is so inaccessible and isolated that considerable effort is required merely to get to where one might like to go. This

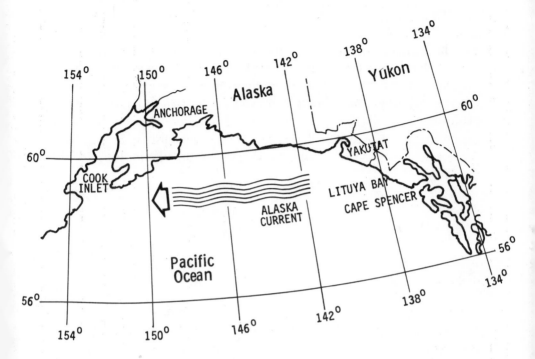

Map 8. Glacier shore Alaska coastline

region is about the most inaccessible of any around the North Pacific Rim, and thus is the least traveled.

Prime Areas

One of the better areas runs from Cape Spencer to Yakutat. There are stretches of exposed drift-laden beaches that will appeal to any beachcomber. At Yakutat there is an excellent beach running east for about 20 miles. Military personnel assigned there have sent many a glass float home. On a beach west of Yakutat is a beachcomber's dream—an old sailing ship standing upright with masts intact, sanded in about 50 yards from the water's edge. The variety of beachcombed items on these isolated shores differs little from what is found on the Oregon coast, except, of course, for the addition of local material.

Alaskan Peninsula

This region is defined as extending from Cook Inlet westward for about 1,000 miles, including the Kodiak Island group on the one side and the Pribilof Islands on the other. The common denominator of this far-flung rugged region is its bad weather. Its occasional sandy beaches collect a wide variety of ocean drift, not from any main ocean current but from the Alaska and Arctic Currents that border the peninsula.

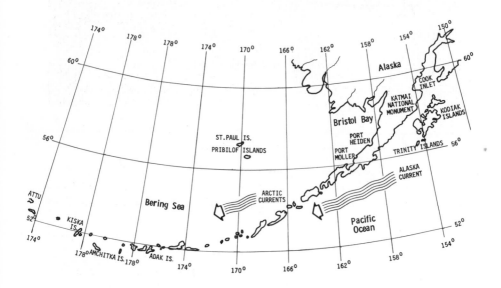

Map 9. Alaskan Peninsula coastline

Regulations

No special restrictions are in force in this region for the beach-comber other than specific government restrictions over the Katmai National Monument, national forests, and wildlife refuges.

Special Conditions

The dangers of beachcombing are equal to the dangers of survival in this part of the world.

Special Equipment

No special equipment is required for beachcombing in this region other than what has already been outlined above as requirements for normal outdoor travel.

This overnight beachcombing campsite alongside the Sandpiper *float airplane is east of Dillingham, Alaska, in Bristol Bay (Dick Hamlin Photo)*

Relative Value

As a beachcombing territory, the Alaskan Peninsula also rates high. No more remote an area borders the North Pacific Rim. The shorelands might be uninhabited for miles upon miles at a stretch, so the population on any beach is apt to be zero. Accessibility to almost any beach is a major problem without the use of aircraft. However, there has been more traffic here in recent years because of oil exploration, much of which is done by helicopter. The few hunters, fishermen, trappers, government residents, and others who earn their living along these shores have some of the finest beachcombing in the world.

Prime Areas

In the Kodiak Island group, one of the better places is on the Trinity Islands at the south end. Here glass fishing floats of all sizes and shapes are picked up following the favorable storms. In the Pribilof Islands, the residents of St. Paul Island have found a wide variety of fishing gear, floats, pieces of ships, and ivory.

On the Alaskan Peninsula along the Bristol Bay side, the Port

Viewed along the high tide line near Port Heiden, Alaska, is this typical beach scene of a basketball-sized crab pot marker float, several orange-sized salmon gill net floats, crates, boxes and other beach debris. (Dick Hamlin Photo)

Heiden and Port Moller areas are well known to local fishermen and hunters for the thousands of Japanese glass fishing floats. These are lined up in a long row at the high tide line and extend for miles, all lost from extensive Bristol Bay Japanese salmon gill net operations. Sometimes fierce winds roll these floats inland for hundreds of yards over sand dunes. Port Heiden is my choice for the last in my list of four best beachcombing spots along the North Pacific Rim.

Further west along the Aleutian Chain, government people assigned to locations such as Adak, Amchitka, Kiska, and Attu locate beachcombable areas. Here are glass floats of all descriptions, ivory, and other Pacific Ocean debris.

Hawaiian Islands

Strategically located 2,400 miles southwest from San Francisco, our fiftieth state is the popular tourist resort for people from all sides of the Pacific Rim. Flights from many points of the compass have destinations at Honolulu on Oahu Island and Hilo on Hawaii Island. Commuter airlines can fly you to other islands in a matter of minutes. With readily available car rental, access to most beaches is no problem.

The Hawaiian Islands are 600 miles north of the westbound North Equatorial Current, thus very little drift carried along in this Pacific Ocean current makes its way to these shores. The islands experience northeast trade winds except for a short period in the winter

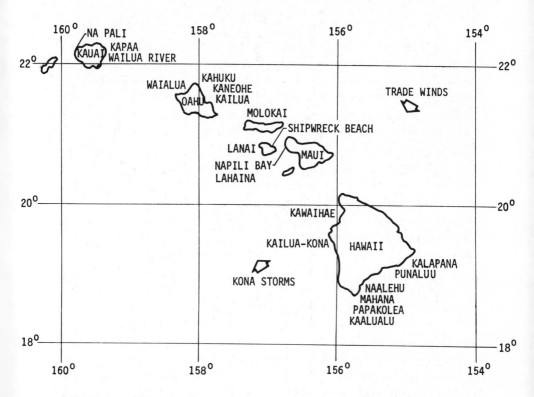

Map 10. Hawaiian Islands

months when Kona storms from the southeast will bring in flotsam from the North Equatorial Current. The trade winds throughout most of the year bring in a modest number of Japanese glass floats on many beaches. Since the Hawaiian Islands experience only small tide changes, the items to be beachcombed will not be as dramatic as, for example, on Oregon's shores. Many of the beaches are inside coral reefs, thus making coral one of the most common beachcombing finds.

Regulations

There are numerous beach parks and campgrounds bordering the public beaches. Camping at beach parks is a popular year-round activity; however, camping permits must be obtained.

Special Conditions

All of the six main islands have their own characteristic mixture of lava beds, steep cliffs, and sand beach shorelines. At certain locations are dangerous beaches, slippery rocks, steep bluffs, and flat tidal areas subject to sneaker waves—as found on our own western Pacific coast. At certain times, beaches may be taboo for swimming because of sharks and devilfish.

Special Equipment

For beachcombing here, a bamboo cane walking stick would be helpful in climbing rocks. A rucksack is necessary since most beaches have coral and shells. When scuba diving, there is much to collect such as black coral, fan coral, shells, and shellfish. If you just want to look, use a glass bottom box. Small plastic pill containers would be desirable to obtain samples of the different colored sands that are encountered.

As for clothing, be prepared for 85-degree daytime temperatures with bright sun and a rainstorm thrown in. The rain, however, never seems to be a bother since everything will dry in a hurry. For beachcombing with its occasional rock climbing, tennis shoes are a must. Bermuda shorts are standard wear, but slacks are better for beachcomber knee protection. All clothing should be loose to prevent heat rash. Shirts should have open necks and elbow length sleeves. A wide-brimmed hat, suntan lotion, and sunglasses complete the outfit and give the beachcomber tourist proper sun protection. This is no small concern; the sun reflects on the white beach sand, thus one gets it from several directions.

Relative Value

As a beachcombing territory, the Hawaiian Islands certainly get about the highest marks for delightful weather and pleasant surroundings. The actual beachcombing gets an average rating, however, principally because of the high population of the region and the dearth of ocean drift. If shells and coral are sought after, then Hawaii gets high marks. These are unique to the islands and are always of interest to the tourist. Shells can be found at many beaches merely for the effort of a short drive or walk. Residents beachcomb for the many varieties of seaweed, most of which are edible. Candlenut seeds with their high percentage of oil are gathered along the beaches in place of firewood because they make a good cooking fire.

Prime Areas

The prevailing northeast trade winds tend to favor the windward sides of the islands during most of the year. Here are the better areas, assuming that the beach configuration will provide for wind-blown items to stay. Where a lava bed or cliff faces that direction, many a bottle or glass fishing float is broken when dashed against the rocks.

Hawaii, the Big Island, has many excellent beaches. There is a 40-mile stretch of white sand beach and lava bed shores along the west coast running north from Kailua-Kona to Kawaihae. One of the best-known beachcombing areas is Kaalualu on the southern shore, which, incidentally, is the southernmost beach in the United States. Here beachcombing for Japanese glass fishing floats has become a popular sport for residents and tourists alike. This beach is accessible from the South Point road, which is improved except for the last quarter-mile.

In this four-mile area, running east toward Naalehu, glass floats are often found on top of the washed sugar cane trash collected along the edge of the tide line. This cane pulp, called *bagasse*, is jammed in by the waves to a height of several feet and a width of about eight feet. It is wedged together so tightly that it has to be cut with a saw, and it is so strong that one can easily walk along the top. This cane comes from the cane fields on the east side of the island.

There are also low rocky headlands here, thus many floats, both glass and plastic, get destroyed, as evidenced by the broken pieces found along the shoreline—the result of savage wave action. The winter months are the best time for this beach. Glass floats, bottles, and plastic buoys are plentiful during this season, blown in during Kona storms from the North Equatorial Current. Many of the larger glass floats are picked up at sea. Few shells and fewer logs are found here.

Beaches at Papakolea and Mahana have beach sand of olivine (technically, a silicate of magnesium and iron). It is emerald green and sparkles like broken up green glass. A sample of this sand in a pill container provides a unique memento of this beach. Further north, black beach sand can be found at Kalapana and Punaluu.

On Maui, the Valley Isle, the west coast is almost a continuous stretch of beach sand. Other portions of the island are dotted with beach coves. Many good western beaches from Lahaina to Napili Bay will yield curios for the tourist. At certain beaches, residents can find Hawaiian diamonds. These are small irregularly shaped stones that have an exterior brown bark—inside they are clear. These diamonds are believed to come from lava beds and were washed down to the beach. Maui is known for its extensive and numerous beaches. One may walk along for miles yet see few people. The rain in the evening is a daily occurrence.

Lanai, the Pineapple Isle, has a 20-mile long shore along the northeast windward coast that is a beachcomber's delight. Here on the northern shore is Shipwreck Beach where several ship hulls lie, some of which were abandoned. Glass floats, pieces of ship timbers, and shells are found along this coast.

Molokai, the Friendly Isle, runs east and west. There are no reefs off the north windward shore of narrow stony beaches and steep cliffs, thus there are few sandy areas. The south shore has occasional sand beaches but little is found here. The few beaches at the west end are not open to the public.

On Oahu, the Gathering Place, one of the beaches that yields a great deal of flotsam is Kailua, almost directly across the island from Honolulu. This bay is all sand, and it is protected by reefs that reduce wave action. Residents who live near the bay have extensive collections of glass fishing floats beachcombed during the winter months of Kona winds. Beaches in this area are of fine sand and are barren of debris. Shells are found on windward beaches going north from Kaneohe and on the north coast from Kahuku to Waialua.

On Kauai, the Garden Isle, one finds one of the better places to beachcomb for glass floats, shells, and coral. Along the east coast between the mouth of Wailua River and Kapaa is an excellent beach for floats. Floats will often be lodged in the pandanus (screw pine) roots. The backyards of many homes near here have glass floats stacked like cordwood; many of them are marked and have nettings.

This sandy beach has a wide variety of tide pools—something

for people of all ages. One can spend a whole day on a half-mile stretch. This beach is readily accessible, has a high yield, and has universal appeal. It is an easily walked beach, although not overly wide.

This is primarily an all-coral sand beach protected by reefs, which result in the wave action being slight. There are places where the pandanus trees grow out of the banks over into the water; if a wave does come in, one merely has to climb up into the branches to wait for the water to subside. This beach faces the trade winds fifty weeks of the year, which accounts for the steady beach yield. December is the best month, but winter is generally good. Coral and shells are in abundance here.

A nurse beachcombing by motorbike at Ahakini near the airport found a bottle with a note inside written in Russian. It had been cast from a fishing vessel during a storm off the Pribilof Islands near Alaska three years earlier. The probable journey of the bottle matched the average speeds of the Kuroshio, California, and North Equatorial Currents, resulting in a 6,000 mile voyage. She has found over 100 glass floats; also boxes, bottles, and other objects covered with gooseneck barnacles.

Many other beaches along the southern and northern shore of Kauai beckon the beachcomber. Because of high cliffs, the northwestern beaches of Na Pali are inaccessible except by boat or helicopter. About forty percent of Kauai's shoreline consists of sandy beaches.

Extending westward from these main islands in a chain over 800 miles long is the Hawaiian Island Natural Wildlife Refuge. This consists of a series of small islands and atolls containing some of the greatest sea bird nesting colonies of the world. The remoteness of this refuge and its difficulty of access provide protection for many species of sea birds and wildlife that frequent this region of the Pacific. The only habitation is at French Frigate Shoals on Tern Island, not much bigger than its runway, where the Coast Guard operates a navigation station.

Terminating at the west end of the refuge is Midway Island, which actually consists of two small islands surrounded by a low reef. Here with strong southeast or northwest winds, glass floats, saki bottles, and other selected debris are washed ashore through openings or over lower portions of the reef. Six miles of beach are thoroughly combed night and day by military people assigned here, since beachcombing is a local popular pastime. Few regulations and fewer dangers limit them in this beach activity. In the normal eighteen-month tour of duty, the average beachcomber will collect about 150 glass floats, plus an occasional oddity like a red clay jug or a bottle containing a note.

Non-beach Beachcombing

Because of the volcanic and mountainous terrain of the Hawaiian Islands, there is little freshwater beachcombing to be done here. Much of the land of the islands is under cultivation, and the rest consists of volcanic material, overgrown jungle valleys, or mountains of dramatic silhouette.

Marshall Islands

This mid-Pacific island group is of special interest to the ocean beachcomber because of its strategic location within a major global ocean current. Since these islands are directly in the path of the speedy westbound North Equatorial Current, the longest current of the northern Pacific circulation pattern, ocean-borne flotsam must first filter through the Marshall Island group. Located in the tenth latitude about halfway between Hawaii and the Philippines, the reefs and beaches of these islands act like a giant sieve that catches ocean debris; thus the Marshalls become a prime beachcombing territory of the Pacific.

Regulations

The Marshall Islands are a part of the United Nations Trust Territory of the Pacific Islands. The United States is the administrator of this group. Travel to many areas is restricted, and written permission is required of the Trust Territory government for any travel beyond designated areas.

Special Conditions

Many islands within atolls here that may look promising for beachcombing must be bypassed because of the risk involved in landing small craft. Fast currents and sizable swells in conjunction with

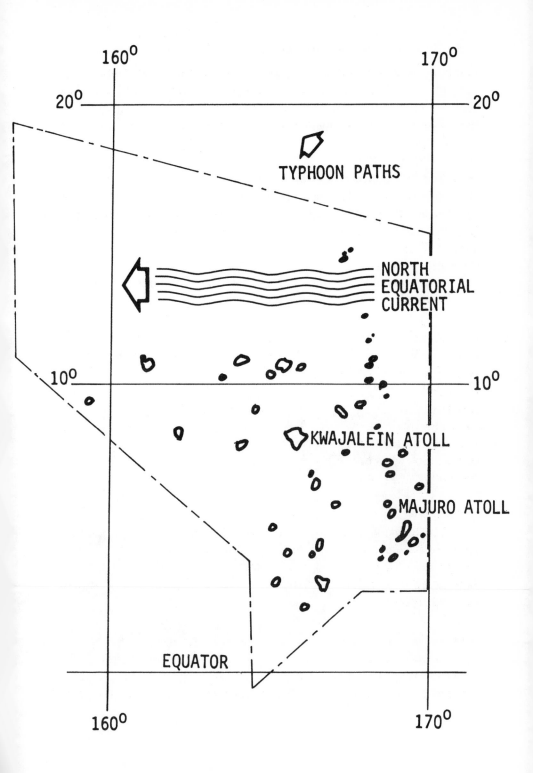

Map 11. Marshall Islands

razor sharp coral formations are dangers to be met whether you are in an inflatable raft or planked boat. These islands also experience typhoon weather that plays havoc with the copra (the dried kernel of the coconut used to produce coconut oil) plantations.

Special Equipment

The first concern is to have adequate clothing and footwear for this tropical region. Travel by boat should be done only with a guide or someone who is thoroughly familiar with the peculiarities of this region.

Relative Value

The Marshalls are one of the better beachcombing territories of the Pacific, principally because of their mid-current geographical location. However, there is competition for beachcombed material; some of the native population is in the commercial beachcombed goods business. The distance to the Marshalls is also a negative factor, especially when weighing the possible return on investment. Travel to individual islands of the atolls is uncertain and risky.

Oriental long line tuna fishing floats and shells beachcombed on Marshall Island beaches. (Richard A. Wasson Photos)

Prime Areas

Natives at places open to tourist travel, such as Majuro Atoll, have giant piles of glass floats for sale that they have gathered from the beaches of the outer islands of the atoll. The Kwajalein Atoll is also a good depository for ocean drift items such as netted glass floats from long line tuna operations, life preservers, lobster pot markers, bottles, and scientific gear. A wide variety of beach coral and shells can also be collected.

Non-beach Beachcombing

The typical Marshall Island atoll consists of a chain of small linear islands often not much wider than the coral beaches of both sides, so there is little opportunity here for inland or upland combing.

Caroline Islands

West of the Marshalls and toward the Philippines, the Caroline Island group of more than 930 islands is strung out over a distance of about 1,800 miles. This far-flung region between the equator and tenth north latitude is also part of the United Nations Trust Territory of the Pacific Islands administered by the United States. The Carolines comprise the four administrative districts of Palau, Yap, Truk, and Ponape. The Carolines, like the Marshalls, are an important interface

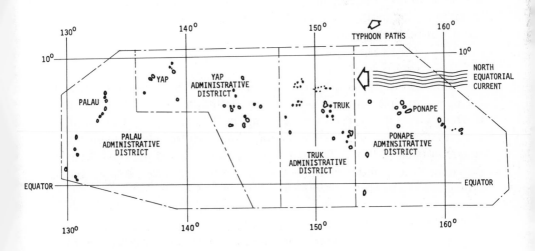

Map 12. Caroline Islands

with the westbound North Equatorial Current of the northern Pacific circulation pattern; consequently this island group is also of interest to the Pacific beachcomber. Debris that floats through the Marshall Islands network has a good chance of being beached in the Carolines.

Regulations

There is no specific regulation or law pertaining to beach-combing as such in the Palau District. There are various marine fishing, tourist, and beautification laws that could be interpreted to cover the subject of beachcombing. For any systematic beachcombing on Palau, a permit should be obtained from the Palau District Administrator.

Special Conditions

These islands with their tropical climate experience an annual rainfall of over 100 inches. Typhoons are common in the northwest area, so weather patterns must be regarded seriously and watched. Some islands, such as Yap, have extensive growth down onto the water's edge, so a beach to catch debris does not exist.

Special Equipment

Here, as on any of the island groups mentioned above, one must first be clothed in accordance with recommended tropic apparel. No special beachcombing equipment is required as long as boat transportation has been arranged.

Relative Value

The Carolines as a beachcombing territory have a good rating because they, too, are directly in the westbound North Equatorial Current. Glass floats have been arriving on Palauan shores for several decades. Japanese and Okinawan long line tuna vessels frequent the waters outside the reef. The natives who have picked up glass floats and stored them under their houses for future sale have accumulated extensive collections.

Prime Areas

The beaches near Kuror on Palau are a recommended place to

start, assuming that favorable weather conditions prevail.

Marianas Islands

Located 1,500 miles east of the Philippine Islands and 900 miles south of Japan in the midwestern Pacific Ocean is this group of fourteen islands plus other islets and reefs—the last of our twelve Pacific Ocean territories. This scene of extensive military operations during World War II, by both Japan and the United States, shows its scars and reminders of a massive engagement. Leftover military tonnage still marks the beaches, harbors show their sunken ships, and even the airfields maintain their own special brand of cast-off military equipment.

Beachcombing here might consist of searching for war souvenirs, but Pacific Ocean flotsam also is continually cast onto some of the islands' flat sandy beaches. Despite the metal and rubber remains of military trucks, landing craft, and personnel gear strewn about on some of the beaches, the ocean still sends in Japanese glass fishing

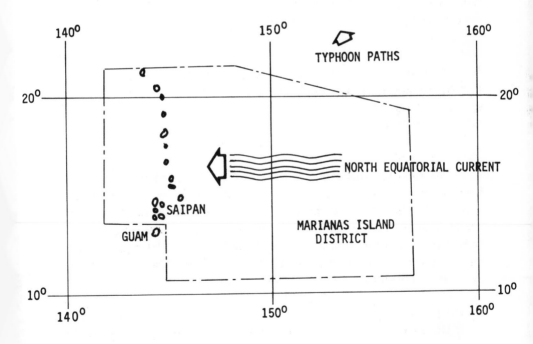

Map 13. Marianas Islands

floats and other flotsam as it did prior to the military invasion of 1944.

Regulations

The United Nations Trust Territory of the Pacific Islands governs all activities here and approval should be obtained from proper authorities prior to random beach travel.

Special Conditions

There should be no reason to encounter any specific dangers here, other than to take the recommended precautions for tropical residence and travel as mentioned for the Marshall and Caroline Islands.

Special Equipment

No special beachcombing gear should be required as long as clothing, footwear, and sun protection is consistent with recommended tropical practices.

Relative Value

The Marianas are a good place to beachcomb because of their isolation, low population, and the impingement of the strong westbound North Equatorial Current on their eastern shores. Steady northeast trade winds assist this process.

Prime Areas

Saipan has good beachcombing. Glass floats seem to come in only on the rocky east side of the island at several small coves with sand beaches. This harvest is believed to be caused by the winds and currents that affect the east coast; however, it should be noted that there is a barrier reef on the west side. A popular location is Profile Beach, at one time a more inaccessible cove because of a road washout. The size, color, markings, and oddities of the glass floats found here match the mix found on west coast American shores.

Beachcombing on Guam is poor because of the offshore reefs. Although Guam does not have many beaches, the best of those that do exist are on the southern coast. Access to most of the shoreline is difficult due to the terrain. The shoreline is high, rocky and hazardous to negotiate. Lesser slopes are on the east side.

5
Displaying and Valuing Beach Items

Much of the fun of beachcombing is telling about your findings, sharing the details of the weather and beach conditions, and showing off that special trophy of some previous beach hike. Beachcombers usually want to display their finds in their homes. If home is near the ocean in a cabin, the findings will be located prominently in the main room for all to see. But if home is in a big city, the beach treasures seem to be relegated to a corner of the family room. Items found by youngsters are kept in their bedrooms, and in the home of a demanding housewife, the items are edged toward the garage, basement, or carport for storage.

There is a real challenge for those who desire to display their harvest from the sea properly, for much of what is found is not in itself artistic. Sometimes, in order to best present a beachcombed object, it is desirable to add complimenting items. For example, a driftwood piece can be shown with shells, starfish, or floats. In some circumstances the surface of the object is treated. Interior decorators use beach driftwood to advantage when it fits a mood or an image. The display of beach findings will vary in as many ways as there are people. I have seen beautiful things displayed abominably and ordinary items decorated artfully, even beyond recognition.

Techniques for Display—General Remarks

The techniques employed in displaying beachcombed treasure are not very involved. Simplicity in presentation and in grouping seems to be the rule. Regarding the preservation, varnishing, or painting of beachcombed items, very little of this is done. Sometimes a layer of clear lacquer is added to shells, but usually they are kept clear of embellishment. Different woods that have been bleached on the seacoast present an undesirable exterior upon being varnished. Sometimes a little black paint can be used to touch up the oriental markings on a piece of dunnage, but this must be done with care, lest the exact lettering be violated. Driftwood generally does not lend itself to painting. A driftwood-colored stain might be used to touch up blemishes or to dull bright wood-colored fractures. The weathering of wood, whether it be on the beach or on the side of an old barn, develops into a familiar tone and texture that is lost when the wood is varnished or painted over.

The polishing of beach rocks, agates, and other stones is a very necessary function prior to display. Normally a piece of jasper or

This necklace was made of puka shells beachcombed on Kauai in the Hawaiian Islands (above, right). (David T. Davis Photo)   An abalone shell found on the British Columbia coast contained these large crater-shaped barnacles that add to its artistic appearance (above, left).

This unusual jewelry tray is readily made by gluing half of an oyster shell on top of an overturned cockle shell.

agate in the raw is rather dull in appearance; however, after tumbling and polishing in a rock tumbler, it emerges with a high luster. The polishing of glass fishing floats is an accepted practice in that they readily collect a film of grime or dust. A display on a window seat or table will mean regular handling for examination, thus the polished floats will be more attractive.

The cutting or trimming of beach driftwood pieces that are destined for display has to be done with caution. If one needs a firm rule, it would be: Don't ever do it. More often than not, the removal of any portion of the original piece will be immediately registered as, and recognized as, an omission to most viewers. In other words, nature's handicraft patterns are so familiar to us all that almost any deviation is readily noted. If the size of a piece of driftwood is too heavy to bring home, it is generally too heavy to display in one's family room.

As opposed to driftwood, the cutting of certain rocks such as geodes and agates into slices *is* desirable. In this way more people can enjoy the beauty of that particular find. Such slices can be displayed by mounting them vertically on a substantial wooden stand so that the light can come in from behind for added enjoyment.

Although this book does not purport to be a crafts book, the following pages will give you some ideas for the most commonly found and displayed items.

Glass Floats

The glass fishing float found sporadically around the Pacific Ocean is the number one prize of the beachcombing fraternity and consequently is given top billing in a beachcomber's collection. The display possibilities are numerous.

Many countries, including Russia, Korea, China, Japan, and the United States, have manufactured glass floats for use in their fishing industries. However, the oriental handblown float with small bubbles in the glass gives an exceptionally pleasing texture when viewed on the surface or through the glass proper. Some older Japanese floats become tinted by the sun and take on an olive or deep blue color, differing from the usual blue-green shade brought about by the recycling of saki bottles. Glass floats can be larger than a basketball or smaller than a golf ball. The larger floats come primarily from Japanese long line tuna fisheries and are the most sought after for both commercial

Barnacle-laden Japanese glass float found after an early spring storm off the Oregon coast south of Netarts. (Burford Wilkerson Photo)

and private displays. Some floats are not spherical, but cylindrical or stretched at the ends like a sweet potato. These shapes add variety and create an opportunity to accent a grouping. Floats of several sizes make up into natural groupings and, thanks to their built-in highlights, are very attractive.

A few beachcombed glass floats are found wrapped in a manila cord or rope netting. Sometimes barnacles and other sea life attach

Prize-winning Japanese glass float shown at Seaside, Oregon,
Beachcomber Festival (above, left). (Burford Wilkerson
Photo)   Japanese glass fishing floats suspended from ceiling with
nylon fishing line add Pacific Ocean accent to decor of living room
(above, right). (David T. Davis Photo)

themselves to this netting. Since only three percent of the floats ever
found have this netting, these floats are quite rare and consequently
are often hung as they are found with barnacles and sea life still attached, after having been adequately preserved. Floats that have lost
their netting may be shown in gift shops hung in a hammock-like netting made of cotton string, or several may be strung up vertically in a
row with macramé craftwork.

It is best to place glass floats so that the light from the outside
will pick up the color, texture, and shape—perhaps in a window or on
a window seat. Glass floats do not show to advantage when pushed
into a dark corner.

From my experience, each glass float needs to have a glass coast-
er or collar to rest upon, otherwise, when disturbed, a carefully captured float can roll off a table or ledge to break into a thousand
pieces. In our home where we have over one hundred glass floats on
display, each one is adequately constrained, and we have yet to have
one roll away. We have lost two during dusting, so now that is considered a two-man chore for both husband and wife.

Glass floats are effectively displayed with shells, driftwood, and
pieces of cork. A single float, shell, and driftwood branch make a fine
table centerpiece.

A very effective setting in a friend's home is a display of random
sized blue-green floats placed on a white shag rug near the entrance to
their living room.

Glass floats are also displayed outdoors in gardens, on porches, along walks, in garage walls, and in pools. They seem to fit into a variety of display uses, particularly in combination with a piece of fish netting. Glass floats are featured by many restaurants where a marine or Polynesian theme prevails.

The artist has found additional uses for the floats. Some floats have been painted with scenes of the mountains, beaches, and sailing ships. Sometimes pieces of broken floats are melted down into a bowl, tray, or centerpiece. Large glass floats have also been used for lamp bases.

Saki Bottles

A saki bottle is always a welcome addition to a beachcombed display because of its colorful vertical accent. It can be used as a vase for fresh flowers or a dried grass arrangement. Some beachcombed saki bottles have been melted down in a kiln to make attractive conversation piece relish dishes. The larger saki jugs, demijohn size, are attractive by themselves on a patio, in a family room, or in a corner that needs a decorative touch. Their blue color and highlight provide an artful contrast to a wall treatment of brick, cedar, or painted plaster.

A large beachcombed bottle provides wide base for bedroom lamp (above, left).   This interesting shelf arrangement includes a mystery urn. (above, right). (Burford Wilkerson Photo)

Agates and Rocks

Many a beachcombed agate and rock go through the rock tumbling process in preparation for display. Larger agates the size of an egg get their own place of importance. Numerous smaller agates are often shown in a tray or small flat bowl; in this way, they will be kept together but still readily available for handling. One of the most effective ways to display groups of smaller polished agates is in a vertical standing glass jar. Parfait glasses or brandy snifters are often used, and when placed near an outside source of light, the effect is delightful. Using sheets of glass mounted in a one-inch frame, in the manner used for ant farms, is an especially effective way of displaying agates. With agates of roughly the same size, each stone can be seen through as well as apart from the others because of the double glass picture frame.

Beachcombers display their colored rocks in vertical standing glass jars; when the jar is also filled with water, the colors and textures of the stones are accentuated. The experts find display cases of various sizes practical for rocks and agates. Discarded jewelry counter cases are especially useful. For large collections of stones, rocks, and rock specimens, a case of drawers will allow compact storage with ready access. For an outstanding display of an unusual item, a portable lighted display case is best of all.

Special Items

I have several unusual beachcombed trophies that require their own special wall bracket or mounting. With custom-made wall attachments, there is no fear that the unique article will be damaged because of improper stowage or handling. I like to display these special items that I treasure on the walls of my study rather than on shelves. Shelves are generally used for ordinary things; any time an item can be wall mounted, its visibility is increased manyfold.

Driftwood

The main criterion for display of driftwood is size. Pieces larger than about four feet and 100 pounds are often relegated to a driveway edging or the corner of the patio without any further consideration. Smaller pieces that can be carried readily in an automobile will get a

Beachcombed cork fishing float makes a simple and effective candle holder (above, left).   End table lamp made by Ruth Mary Close from plastic float and rocket launcher box beachcombed at Cox Bay, Vancouver Island (above, right).

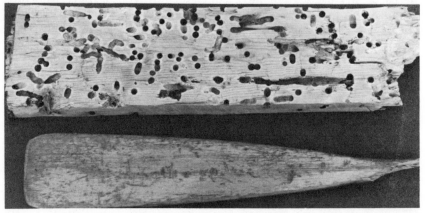

A study of contrasts in beachcombed woods—weatherbeaten cedar wormwood and varnished spruce oar fragment.

great deal more attention. These can be scrubbed, rubbed, and stained to a finish that will contrast beautifully in almost any setting, whether it be table or wall.

Woods that have been eaten away by the teredo or shipworm are also sought after for use in displays. Pieces of piling or planks attacked by these marine borers are sold by the pound because of the demand by craftsmen.

Driftwood branches or limbs often resemble figures of animals or fowl after they have been worked over and tumbled about in the surf. These likenesses are often featured in a number of ways by the finder.

Driftwood Finishing. The finishing of driftwood is an art. I have visited classes where this is taught and learned that beautiful sculptured pieces can be made from root structures, stump parts, burls, and other unusual woody growths. The thrust of this craft is to end up with artistic items suitable for living room use and display. Some are fashioned into delightful wall pieces, others provide table centerpieces in conjunction with glassware or shells.

Samples of artistic driftwood pieces found on the outer coast of Vancouver Island near Nootka, British Columbia.

The dean of class instruction in the Pacific Northwest for this art work is Mrs. Lucille Worlund of Bellevue, Washington, who has developed an approach known as the Luron method. Her procedure is first to clean and remove all dirt and decayed portions, then to provide a work hardened surface, and finally to add an oil finish. Her unique approach results in some of the most exquisite pieces yet created, as shown by the fact that her students win the top honors at shows.

This creativity is guided by principles that require hand work only. No power tools for wood surface conditioning. No wax or filler finishes, only light oil rubbing. No staining.

Because these pieces are labors of love, often taking many hours of tedious and painstaking effort to achieve high quality, they are rarely for sale. No two pieces are alike; each is the personal project of the student.

Many of these pieces come from upland mountain lakes and streams, rather than from an ocean beach directly. Most driftwood gathered for artistic qualities will be in better condition at the source of supply; after the torturous trip down valley and over waterfall to the ocean and finally through the surf, they will be in a battered condition. However, many burls and other unusual growths ride through to beach drift piles in relatively protected condition.

A recommended technique for the finishing of a burl is to oil it with salad oil all over first and allow it to soak for three months. This loosens all the pitch. Second, scrape with a chisel and sandpaper to clean off any and all loose pieces. This step brings out the surface texture and grain of the wood. The final surface polishing consists of: (1) oiling with a furniture polish; (2) honing with a deer antler horn; (3) polishing with a lemon wax; and (4) final honing with a deer horn.

Collages

Many dedicated beach craftsmen have turned to the artistic expression of collages. These artistic compositions are an assemblage of beach drift fragments glued to a flat surface. Some are miniature size for wall use, others consist of panels large enough for hallway or foyer decoration. Many beach homes have large panel collages as wind breaks, or as carport or fence decorations.

The driftwood collage, a relatively new art form, has widespread popularity and is being readily accepted for wall decoration use, not only in the home, but in public building, industrial, and commercial office decor as well. The market for these interestingly textured wall pieces has favored the seller.

To make a driftwood collage, it is first necessary to establish the size category of the items to be collated. Then beachcomb for the individual pieces of wood, bark, shells, coral, and other shore bric-a-brac that are to make up the general theme you have in mind. Bits of wood no longer than a pencil and as short as a paper clip that have been tumbled in the surf provide excellent materials for collages. Then, after you have acquired several shoe boxes full of beach debris, spread them out on a table, sand and all, and separate into three piles —usable, questionable, and probably not usable. If the first two piles appear to contain more than enough material to construct your project, then clean and polish each item in these piles. Next, select or grade your items into categories by appearance: plain or fill-ins; art forms; art form framers; accents; textures of bark; and terredo. Now begins the design process, which requires that good composition be accomplished if you hope to place in the beachcomber festival competitions. The way the pieces are placed, almost jigsaw fashion, will establish the intended image and incidentally reflect some of your own personality. It will certainly be your own creation.

For gluing on the individual pieces, use an all-purpose casein base household glue or thickened wood glue. The backing board may be covered with burlap or drapery fabric of a contrasting texture; in this way, the burlap will act as the border matting around the collage. It might be desirable to make this border several inches wide in both directions.

Some driftwood collages are multilayered. The first layer attached to the backing board might be pieces that are basically plain or background items. A second layer might consist of complementing pieces to the third and outer layer that would consist primarily of the design image pieces and accents. Arrangement of the pieces for layers two and three have to be developed together.

Be sure to select larger individual pieces, even up to twelve inches long, if the collage is to be used outdoors—because it will be viewed from a greater distance away. Also be sure to use waterproof glue. Driftwood used outdoors, whether used in collages or alone, should be left unworked and untreated because the polish or varnish will invariably weather to an unsightly appearance. Many a successful outdoor collage has been constructed of shells, cork floats, foam plastic, fishing gear, bottles, light bulbs, and broken pieces of planking —things that by themselves have a mundane look—without any other treatment. Often a fishing net will be draped or used as a wall hanging on which beach drift items have been secured.

For collages aimed at interior display, there is the opportunity of a greater variety in form. A more delicately designed collage can thus be created. Some are free hanging, many vertically mounted, and others are horizontally directioned. Some have conventional frames. Others have been fashioned on an old piece of flat wood with roughened edges, which likewise had experienced the wave and surf tumbling treatment. Some collages are three-dimensional, like mobiles.

Mobiles

Anyone creating a mobile from beach drift items automatically has a conversation piece. One need not follow any prescribed pattern in the design. The lateral arms can be thin lengths of root driftwood, even dried out pieces of kelp, which, when dried, become surprisingly stiff and take on interesting shapes. The objects to be suspended can be small shells, dried out tidal life forms, bits of wood, rocks, frosted beach glass, agate, or whatever suits one's fancy. Small pieces of drift- wood that might have an eye at one end making them resemble small fish, can be strung to imitate the swimming motions of goldfish in a bowl. Salmon fishing plug lures make lifelike representations of swim- ming fish when suspended in the same manner. The smaller sized Jap- anese glass fishing floats have also been used either alone or in con- junction with other items. The design of a mobile should take into consideration the weights of the different objects to be suspended and their relationship during the wind created movements. Those who want to construct an outstanding beach drift mobile would do well to follow one of the classic and established patterns already designed by professionals.

Valuation

All beachcombed material has intrinsic value, even though some people merely look for a small item that will remind them later on of the carefree walk on that particular occasion. Some beachcombers immediately can put a value on what is picked up. Many a shell is readily available on almost any Pacific beach for the picking up; yet, when a few other beach drift bits are glued into place in combination with this single shell, it may sell for $2.50 at a nearby gift shop. Even so, the purchaser will get a fine bargain because he will not have to take the time to do all the searching and craftwork involved.

Nature-made objects are usually harder to price than man-made items. An agate on the beach is not easily priced, while a fifty-foot piece of man-made nylon line has a specific value because this can be assigned a percentage salvage value based on an original catalogue price list.

Estimates of dollar value for a few beachcombed items of man-made origin found on our western Pacific Ocean beaches are given here:

Old bottles	$ 2–$ 20	Crab pot	$ 30
Drift bottles	$ 2–$ 5	Crab pot buoys	$ 2–$ 5
Position bottles	$ 2–$ 5	Lumber ten feet long	$ 1
Saki jugs	$ 20	Nameplates	$ 2–$ 5
Ginger jars	$ 5–$ 10	Oriental crates	$ 2–$ 5
Glass floats	$0.50–$100	Hatch covers	$ 15
Plastic floats	$ 1–$ 5	Life rings	$ 5–$ 15
Steel floats	$ 2–$ 5	Scientific gear	$10–$500
Nylon nets	$ 1–$100	Mystery jugs	$50–$100
Bamboo trays	$ 10–$ 20	Gold coins	$10–$300

Even though the Japanese glass fishing float drifts ashore all around the shores of the North Pacific Rim, it is the favorite of the beachcomber. The vacationing couple from Lincoln, Nebraska, who find a Japanese glass float on the beach at Lincoln City, Oregon, will certainly plan to display it in their front room. If they do not find one, they will want to buy one from the nearby gift shop. Thus, some people want to buy these treasures from others who have found more than they need. Some years the harvest of glass floats on the Oregon coast is not enough to meet tourist demands, so shop owners will import glass floats found in Alaska.

Pacific coast beach gift shop asking prices for these fishing floats closely mirror the market that exists. The gift shop owner knows what the market will bear and he will revise the prices accordingly. If the prices are too high, the merchandise does not move. If they are too low, everything sells out fast. Prices for the different sizes of glass floats are generally related to diameter.

As to average asking prices, some people follow the common rule of one dollar per inch of diameter. This is an easy measure to use on the different sizes, but not very many gift shops follow this rule due to the market that exists.

Certain sizes of floats are found less often than others, so these are more scarce. To help explain this I developed a scarcity index based on actual findings. This index was established by assigning a unit of one to the most commonly found float sizes. Thus, larger or smaller floats that are found less frequently will have a scarcity index with a number larger than one. For example, the scarcity index for an eleven-inch diameter float is twenty-seven, meaning that, on the average, one would beachcomb twenty-seven floats of the commonly found size for every single float of this large size.

With this in mind, I obtained a wholesale price list from a Japanese glass float manufacturer for the different sizes. By comparing these factory prices with gift shop asking prices and including the scarcity index, I then determined a theoretical value for each size float. This interesting comparison is shown below:

	Japanese Glass Float Price List			USA Beachcombed Float Asking Prices		
				Giftshop		
Catalogue Ball No.	Diameter in Inches	Price (Yen)	Price ($)	Asking Price ($)	Scarcity Index	Theoretical Value ($)
1.5	1¾	8.00	.022	.50	27	27.00
1.8	2⅛	8.00	.022	.50	27	27.00
2.0	2⅜	8.00	.022	.75	27	27.00
2.2	2⅝	8.30	.023	.75	14	14.00
2.5	3	9.50	.026	1.00	1	1.00
2.6	3⅛	9.50	.026	1.00	1	1.00
2.8	3⅜	10.50	.029	1.00	1	1.00
3.0	3½	12.20	.032	1.00	1	1.00
3.5	4⅝	17.30	.048	2.00	1.5	1.50

4.0	4¾	22.90	.064	2.00	2.8	2.80
5.0	5¾	46.00	.13	3.00	6.8	6.80
6.0	7⅛	70.00	.20	5.00	8	8.00
7.0	8¼	88.00	.25	8.00	9	9.00
8.0	9⅜	105.00	.29	10.00	10	10.00
9.0	10⅝	126.00	.35	20.00	16	16.00
10.0	11¾	150.00	.42	25.00	20	20.00
11.0	13	174.00	.48	30.00	27	27.00
12.0	14¼	210.00	.58	40.00	40	40.00
13.0	15¼	300.00	.84	50.00	54	54.00
15.0	17⅞	750.00	2.08	100.00	250	250.00

There are always those one-of-a-kind items that beachcombers will come across that defy the marketing process. A woman near San Diego, California, found an authentic figurehead from the prow of a Polynesian war canoe. A resident on Vancouver Island, British Columbia, picked up an ivory Nootkan Indian war club. A 600-page log book beautifully handwritten in Spanish was found by a teenage boy in the driftwood on the Washington coast. A medallion given to an Indian chief by the famous British explorer Captain Cook during a visit in 1778 to the Pacific Northwest coast was found in recent years by an Indian on a Vancouver Island beach. A red flag with Japanese lettering from a Japanese fishing boat was found on the Pribilof Islands, Alaska, by a resident there. A ceremonial flower vase from a Buddhist temple in Japan was picked out of the oyster beds of Hood Canal, an inlet of Washington State. A silver bowl of Dutch manufacture, circa 1750, was dug out of the sand on the Oregon coast. These are just a few examples of the many unusual items that are cast up by the Pacific.

All of the foregoing items are truly museum pieces and treasures in themselves. Most of these have no price—nor does a price tag accompany the sand dollar shell that the tourist finds on a California beach.

Beachcomber Fairs

Mention should be given to some of the beachcomber fairs and displays that take place along the Pacific Ocean coast. Beachcombers occasionally like to show their findings and compare them with what

Largest Japanese float displayed at the 1973 Netarts, Oregon, Beachcombers Fair. (Bert Webber Photo)

others have found elsewhere. As a rule, beachcombers do not seem to be individuals who form clubs with an organized social overtone. They are often beach community residents who will readily talk of their finds but who are not the least bit interested in organizing an activity around their beachcombing efforts. Since beachcombing is an individual activity, this may explain the tendency to steer away from an organized group. Incidentally, I have yet to hear of a single club that has been formed around beachcombing pursuits.

There are several regional beachcomber fairs now held annually in the vicinity of Pacific Northwest ocean beach communities. The mere location of these fairs may reflect the peak of Pacific coast

Bert Webber shows drain plug from oriental wooden barrel displayed at the 1973 Netarts Beachcombers Fair. (Dale Webber Photo)

beachcombing. They take place from Grayland, Washington, on the north, to Bandon, Oregon, at the south.

The Grayland show is generally held in February or March in the Grayland Community Hall and is billed as "The Beachcombers Driftwood Show." Begun in 1964, it is sponsored by the Twin Harbors Beach Association. The different categories are listed as follows: collages, wall pieces, driftwood and/or shell pictures, whimsies, functional, decorative, miniatures, diminutives under four inches, glass and floats, foreign bottles. There is a separate competition for flower arrangements for adults and juniors. One of their show rules is that the driftwood may be gathered from beach, stream, lake, field, or forest.

Paul Schafer displays prize-winning upright spinning wheel he designed and built from various hardwoods beachcombed from Oregon beaches.

The Seaside, Oregon, Beachcombers Festival was established in 1969 as a wintertime activity to complement their full summer schedule. It is held on Washington's Birthday weekend and is sponsored by the Seaside Chamber of Commerce. The categories are: driftwood, floats, rocks, shells, wall hangings, bottles, and potpourri. A recent show drew some 3,000 people to view more than 175 exhibits in Seaside's new Civic Convention Center. A major attraction was the nine special demonstrators who gave slide shows, performed craftwork, and demonstrated do-it-yourself projects.

The oldest fair is the Beachcombers Fair held at Netarts, Oregon, west of Tillamook. The first one was held in 1960, and it is sponsored by the Beachcombers Chamber of Commerce of Netarts, Oceanside, and Cape Meares. It is usually held at the height of the beachcombing season in March at the Netarts Fire Hall. The committee also has organized a wide variety of classifications for entries: float collections, collages, bottles, agates, driftwood, table arrangements, animal likenesses, mobiles, lamps, photographs, and flotsam and jetsam.

In the fall a show is held at Bandon, Oregon, in conjunction with their Cranberry Festival.

6
Safety

For most of us, the treasures and pleasures of beachcombing leisure are special vacation experiences of abandonment, whether it be one's meanderings alone down a deserted sandy coastal beach or on a beachcombing treasure hunt with a group. We don't wish to be governed by any rules because that is why we go to the beach in the first place, namely to escape the regulated existence of daily responsibilities and our keyboard culture.

A few of us who spend numerous hours on the beach and those who live in the immediate proximity of the beach have learned some of the behavioral secrets of the sea. Portions of this information can be disconcerting. The Pacific Ocean is an exacting body of water. On occasion it relieves pent-up energies, seemingly in order to keep both sides of the mathematical equation honest in Mother Nature's account book. Several experiences—some serious, others almost—will be related in the following pages.

Equipment

There are a variety of items of equipment that beachcombers should have in order to accomplish their goals and yet be prepared to meet up with possible emergencies. The right clothing and footwear

177

for the weather expected on that particular day is assumed to have been selected.

When considering items to have available in the car or boat, the first should be a first aid kit. It is generally wrong to assume that there is one in the car you may be driving, so make sure one is available. The next in importance is to have blankets for treatment of shock or exposure.

Awareness of possible emergencies, how to avoid them, and, when necessary, how to meet them are concerns along many Pacific beaches. A friend had occasion to be watching some swimmers in a heavy surf from his car on a road atop a bluff on the Oregon coast. This beach was known to him as one that under certain conditions had an undertow. He noticed a swimmer apparently in trouble being pulled out to sea. My friend hurriedly opened up the trunk of his car, pulled out the spare tire, wheel and all, and rolled it down over the bluff where it bounded out into the water. Floating as it did, it became a temporary life preserver and was instrumental in saving the young man's life. Here was a case in which a little knowledge in the hands of a resourceful person averted a possible beach tragedy. On this occasion the emergency was met, but not based on any general beach equipment list.

BEACH SAFETY RULES
BEACHES ARE STATE RECREATION AREAS
MOTORISTS BEWARE OF LOOSE SAND
DISCHARGING FIREARMS ON BEACHES PROHIBITED BY LAW
DANGER-BEACH LOGS MAY BE MOVED BY WAVE ACTION
BEWARE OF DEEP WATER, SINKHOLES AND OUTGOING TIDES
DUMPING RUBBISH PROHIBITED BY LAW
BUILDING FIRES IN DRIFTWOOD PILES PROHIBITED
ISOLATED SMALL FIRES PERMITTED
ENJOY AND KEEP OUR BEACHES SAFE AND CLEAN
OREGON STATE HIGHWAY COMMISSION

WRECK OF THE PETER IREDA
HERE LIES THE REMAINS OF THE FOUR MAS

Oregon State Highway Division Cadet Patrolman assigned to coastal beach duty displays some of the mobile rescue equipment readily available for beach emergencies (above, left).   Typical sign posted on Oregon coastal beaches clearly states the rules you are expected to follow (above, right). (Oregon State Highway Division Photos)

A thermos of hot tea is always handy after a long day's beach hike, not only to quench one's thirst, but a small amount might also be diverted to wash one's windburned face. This is the sort of thing to have in the car, in the boat, or at the base camp from which you begin your beach hiking activity.

For a long day's hike, I recommend ten beachcombing essentials for the rucksack. These are listed in the order of importance: tide tables, spare socks, canteen of water, lunch, gloves, matches, plastic tarp, camera, fishing line and hooks, and small towel. You may want to add other items such as a jackknife and a police-type whistle, but don't fail to recognize and respect the wisdom of having these beachcombing essentials in your backpack or rucksack. You may have to face the unexpected.

Natural Dangers

Sneaker Waves

Sneaker waves are about the most unpredictable and serious emergency on a flat sandy beach, particularly at low tide. Without warning, a wave of considerable energy can sweep toward the shore for hundreds of yards, picking up everything in its way, raising the water level by ten feet, slamming up against the shore, and leaving everything strewn about. Then there is the sluicing back, the rolling of boom logs, the tumbling of stumps and other shore debris—all the while retreating. Many who have been caught in these tsunami type waves tell me that it is a terrifying experience. Fatalities have occurred from drowning as well as from being crushed between logs.

Sneaker waves occur in many places along the western coastal shores of the Pacific Ocean. At higher latitudes with higher tides, such as in Alaska, a wave can be devastating; at lower latitudes with lower tides, it is still serious. In August 1972, the Roland Baggs family were picnicking with other family friends at Corona del Mar south of Newport Beach, California. From a relatively placid sea condition, and without any warning, a wave swept in that put the entire group to rout. All the beach fires were put out, picnic baskets and blankets were picked up and then floated out into the water. Several hundred people in all were involved, some of whom got doused, but for the most part no real damage occurred except for the experience of having to run away from the oncoming wave. But it might have been serious.

Ocean Beach Logs

Loose logs in and along the drift after a high tide or tsunami are a major concern. Almost every year there are fatalities caused by large logs that have been released from precarious positions and have rolled down to a lower level. A log lying crisscross on another, jack-straw style, is always potentially dangerous. The seasoned beach-comber carries a walking stick, and when he is the first down the beach after a high tide, he can free or trigger such logs, not only for his own safety but also for those who might follow and not be familiar with this booby trap danger. We once found a boom log resting thirty feet above high tide level on a rocky outcropping on the west coast of Vancouver Island, British Columbia. It had been flipped up there months before during a winter storm and had been a hazard all that time—until we pried it off its supporting pivot points.

Slippery logs are a hazard during and after rain. A special source of danger is a green, slimy, almost transparent marine growth on logs that have recently been brought in by the tides. Many a time, when I thought I was sure of my footing, I have been fooled by this growth. Even the cautious beachcomber can slip when traversing a long line of wood drift.

Gloves are an important item to pack in your rucksack in order to prevent your picking up any wood splinters from the chewed up ends of beachwood and logs. It doesn't take long for the surf to bash off the square ends of a log or plank into the familiar elliptical shape.

When walking the drift and while stepping from one log to another, always be certain that the new log is secure. An unsecure log is a dangerous item that can suddenly put you into a compromised position by having other logs topple around your legs.

Dimension lumber often contains nails, and most of the time they are sticking upward. As a rule I avoid walking on any dimension lumber for this very reason. A nice flat piece of wood is always an in-vitation to walk upon, particularly if you have been hiking a dry sand stretch with an unfirm surface. Dimension lumber is found on coastal

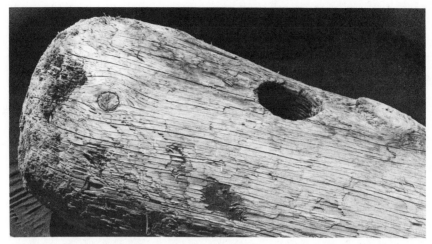

Pacific Ocean beach sand is blown away from the weathered end of a boom log, showing the rounded end that these logs soon acquire.

beaches from California to Alaska; however, it is more prevalent on Oregon and Washington beaches than in British Columbia or Alaska waters due primarily to higher population density. Dimension lumber lost as a deck load from a ship at sea would not contain any nails, but this type of lumber is readily distinguished by the large number of pieces strewn along the high tide line. It is the occasional plank or board torn from a crate by the action of the sea that is to be avoided as a sidewalk. Pieces of broken up boats or random pieces of plywood are always suspect.

Tide Troubles

Know your local tide conditions. Don't get trapped against a steep cliff by a tide. Most of us cannot avoid exposure consequences if forced to hang on a narrow, slippery, wave-swept footing for the six hours that it may take for the tide to turn. One must accept the plain simple fact that, on taking a hike down a beach past a rocky outcropping, there is sure to be a major tide change upon making the return walk. Again, as a general rule, upon passing a point or narrow beach, one must plan on its being closed or covered by the relentless sea upon return.

At Cox Bay near Tofino, British Columbia, an exhausted,

soaked to the skin, barely coherent stranger walked up to the front door of a nearby family beach home asking for help. He had been caught on some rocks as the tide rose and had found it necessary to swim several hundred yards across an inlet to another point to avoid being caught in a high surf to almost certain death. Fortunately this

The driver of this car was driving the beach at low tide near Ocean Park, Washington, when he attempted to cross a small creek. The incoming tide surrounded the car before it could be pulled free. (Hjalmar Brenna Photo)

stranger managed to swim the necessary distance and luckily stumbled into emergency assistance; otherwise, he might have unnecessarily made newspaper headlines.

Also at Cox Bay, there is a tourist cabin resort that caters to those who want to spend a vacation on the ocean beach. On one of our many trips to this beach, we learned of a mystifying experience that had happened a few years before. A city dweller staying at the resort inquired about the position of the tides as he wanted to build a beach fire. The tide table was checked, and it was pointed out that it would be fine to build the fire near the edge of the driftwood since the tide was on its way out. In a very short time he had his fire under way. The young man shortly reappeared and said that the tide had put out his fire. Thinking that he was kidding, a check showed that, sure enough, the tide was full. The tide tables were checked again, and it was considered that they had been misread; after careful checking, he was assured that if he would build his fire again in the same place it would be all right as the tide should be turning. In about an hour he was back to relate somewhat apologetically that they had had a fine fire going but that the tide had again come in and drowned it.

To everyone's complete and utter amazement, the tide had again reached out and touched the high tide mark. By dinnertime a total of twelve high tides had taken place, each more mystifying than its predecessor. After dinner the evening news soon solved the mystery of the strange tides. A disastrous earthquake had taken place off the coast of Chile and its tidal waves had arrived in about fourteen hours to completely override the scheduled tide pattern.

Sandbars

Attractive places to beachcomb are the sandbars that are formed where a river or stream meets the ocean. Here there may be river debris beached downwind on the ocean beaches. However, I must interject a word of caution about sandbars because they can be dangerous for the beachcomber.

The smaller streams spread out and trickle into numerous small shallow channels across the hardened sand beach, and these are not particularly dangerous; however, it is the larger streams that I am talking about. The sandbars formed and the sandbanks eaten away or filled in by the continual erosion or deposition of these larger watercourses look innocent enough, but they can be treacherous. Such recently formed sand beds are readily recognized by the coarser size of the sand particles. As a general rule, wherever the sand appears to be of a fine grain size, as on an ocean beach where the surf constantly pounds away, the footing is sure and the walking easy. Wherever the sand appears to have a coarse grain size, the walking is more laborious and one's footprints penetrate the surface as much as an inch. Watch out for these sand areas regardless of where you may be walking, particularly if you are near a stream bank.

A story from my own experiences should convince you of the wisdom of this advice. One day I was walking an isolated beach on the Washington coast by myself and came to a major stream about forty feet across. It was in flood condition and had a newly formed bank on my side. It was obvious by the depth and velocity of the current that I was not going any further that day. I walked up to the sandbank edge not realizing the potential danger of the freshly deposited coarse-grained sand along the steep banked stream. Before I knew what was happening, the sand gave way beneath my feet and I slid down the side of the bank; I was still going before I had the presence of mind to turn and fall into the bank, grabbing at the sand with the fingers of both hands. Fortunately, with the action of my knees and hands, I was able to crawl up the five-foot bank even though my footing on the bank beneath the water was absolutely nil. There was no footing anywhere on that bank beneath the water. The sand gave way like so many well lubricated marbles stacked on a slope. In fact, that simile is quite accurate; the river had stacked up the sand along the edge like so many tiny marbles. Had the current carried me out to sea, which was a distinct probability in this situation, I, too, might have become a statistic.

Wildlife

Regarding the wildlife that may come down the beach to feed, I believe there is no real concern except for the occasional bear. Most of the other animals seem to keep out of the way. I have, however, gotten pretty close to deer where an onshore wind did not betray my presence. An Alaska beachcomber friend, Dick Hamlin, was trailed along a beach by a wolf, but it seemed as if the wolf was just curious not famished. I have seen lots of cougar tracks, but never any in the making. Although smaller animals and fowl frequently scavenge Pacific shores—including snowy owls at night at the high tide line and eagles and osprey during the day—I have yet to hear of any tragic experiences that have resulted from their activities.

Mention should be made of the story about a mailman who walked a portion of Washington's Pacific Ocean coast years ago and who was chased out into the water by a bear. The mail carrier dropped his mailbag to keep out of the way of the bear. The bear got ahold of the mailbag, and it was reported that people at La Push, Washington, received letters with holes punched through them.

A sea lion stranded on a beach should be given a wide berth. Also, should you happen upon a partly expired sea otter, don't handle it—they bite.

There are a few cautions that should be issued regarding marine life in the tidal zone. The red jellyfish can sting, so watch out. Velellas, cousins to the Portuguese man-of-war, are not dangerous—unlike their Atlantic Ocean counterparts—only slippery to walk on when cast up on the beach after west winds. Rocks in the tidal zone may also be dangerous; some have barnacles, which are exceedingly sharp, and some also have other marine life attached to them that make them slippery to walk on.

Beachcombing with Groups

After reading about the dangers described above, it might seem that the safest way to take a long beach hike to an unfamiliar place would be with a group; however, that is not necessarily so. A large group soon gets strung out. The more adventuresome people start out ahead, while the more experienced beachcombers tend to string out behind. Although the ones ahead usually are the first to get into a beach problem, those behind may be more capable of both avoiding and/or solving it. Even with a small-sized group of four, each member may easily drift away out of shouting distance of the others.

Where a rescue has to take place, the large group usually has the capability of bringing it about. There will be more chance of an organized effort in this direction. Unfortunately, this is not always the case, as evidenced by the following experience. A group of Pacific Ocean beachcombing vacationers had decided to go swimming. Unfortunately a sneaker wave came through and caught the group at different places on the beach. The beach logs were floated and carried down the beach. One of the swimmers was struck. Before any rescue effort could be organized by the others, he disappeared into the outgoing tide.

All members of the group should know the characteristics of the beach to be beachcombed. Watch for the many areas with steep rocks, islands, and sunken jetties—all readily accessible at low tide but isolated at high tide. The waiting at such a spot may not be dangerous, but the uncomfortable hours spent in the elements, with possible effects of exposure, must be reckoned with.

To get this type of information to the group means that someone who knows what is about to be encountered has to assume a leadership role and give a short briefing before the group starts.

Beachcombing with a group of small children has its own set of problems. A friend had taken a group of school classmates for a beach walk, and before she realized it, some of the group had run ahead, out of voice control. On a windy day, this will be only a short distance. Before she could get up to them, four youngsters had crawled up on a large log that was not secure. As it started to roll, three lost their balance and fell free, but before anybody could do anything, the log had rolled over the fourth little girl. The log stopped after rolling over her legs. My friend frantically dug the sand away from under the trapped girl, thus releasing the child from under the log—she was shaken and frightened but unhurt, thanks to the fact that the massive log stopped where it did.

Leaving Word

The intentions of the beachcomber, whether starting with a small or large group, even for a hike that will last for only part of the day, should be shared with all members of the group. This may require that someone climb up on a secure log and get agreement on the activities for that day's hike. Declared destinations, alternates, estimated times for departure, agreed-upon rendezvous places, and estimated times for return—all are simple things to establish. If the base of operations is two parked automobiles and the group splits up into opposite directions, even a short note by the first returning party tucked under the windshield wiper of the other car is a communication courtesy.

There is no more helpless feeling than to learn that a boat containing four beachcombers has not returned to the dock by ten o'clock on a foggy night, especially when it isn't known what they expected to do when they left or when they had expected to return. The matter of assistance becomes frustrating. The fun of beachcombing also starts to wear thin for the four who are stranded on a strange beach all night without matches, food, or cover because one member got lost in the woods while taking a shortcut.

If you are staying at a motel and are going some distance to an island beach that is off the beaten trail, it is easy to tell the manager what your plans are and what to do should you not return by a certain time.

Beaches to Avoid

There are places where the beachcomber should not pursue his hobby. Basically there are four types of places to avoid: government areas closed to the public, Indian reservations, long sloping barren clay banks, and narrow beach areas near steep rocky cliffs.

Closed government lands that border saltwater beaches are usually patrolled, and for good reason. If a civilian beachcomber were to wander unannounced within these federal facilities, his safety might be compromised. Gedney Island, formerly one of our personal favorite beachcombing islands, three miles across from our cabin at Clinton, Washington, was off limits during World War II because this island was used for air-to-ground gunnery practice and dive bombing. Large targets were erected on the northern sand spit for student Air Force pilots to dive at and fire away. Many a weekend during that war while beachcombing Whidbey Island, we could hear machine gun bursts when pursuit airplanes approached these ground targets. Small bombs were also dropped. For years afterward we found machine gun

Not all beaches are flat and sandy, allowing ocean drift to collect. This photo of the rock-bound coast of Washington shows an area to avoid because of steep cliffs and the low likelihood of finding any beach treasure. (Weldon W. Rau Photo)

A dramatic example of the most dangerous of beaches—this photo taken in northern Washington. (Weldon W. Rau Photo)

cartridge cases and an occasional dummy practice bomb shell on our side of Whidbey Island.

A second area to watch out for is the posted Indian reservation. In recent years, several of the Pacific Northwest reservations have been violated by white people's debris and fires, so the Indians put a stop to this trespassing. They began patrolling their domain with jeeps driven by their own deputies. If the trespassing was innocent, you would be asked politely to leave; if the intent was more serious, then you would be issued a summons. The right of the Indian to all beached items within the reservation is traditional and historic. Their livelihood has for centuries depended upon the shellfish and other edibles gathered from the beach; thus they have prior claim to everything there, including any debris, flotsam or cargo from ships, or other salvage. As an example, in 1878 during the construction of the lifesaving station, the McCurdy family was living at Neah Bay near Cape Flattery, on the Makah Tribe Indian Reservation. Young Jimmy McCurdy joined his Indian friends in the beachcombing of milled lumber and miscellaneous cargo jettisoned from some sailing ship during a storm. He quickly found out, with a threat on his life, that whatever came into the beach belonged to the Indians there, and to no one else.

Clay banks with high slopes are particularly treacherous for the beachcomber to descend in bad weather. No matter how inviting a beach may appear from several hundred feet up, accidentally falling or sliding all the way down out of control at a good rate of speed with nothing to slow you down into driftwood at the bottom would court disaster. There is a beautiful beach in Oregon near Cape Blanco that is readily accessible from the top, but one look down that clay bluff on a wet rainy morning was enough for me. Instead, we drove several miles to the north where we could easily reach a different beach.

Long, narrow beaches along steep rocky cliffs are places I avoid unless I know the tide pattern for that particular day. There is an enticing narrow beach area in Washington, north of the Columbia River, where there have been numerous instances of people getting stranded on the rocky banks during a rising tide and pounding surf. Attempts to climb the rocks have often failed, thus requiring Coast Guard rescue. Some rocky outcroppings with no beaches require hiking over headlands, which along the Pacific Northwest coast often means fighting one's way through dense underbrush. There are still miles and miles of other beaches better suited to Sunday afternoon beachcombing with all the attendant amenities, so not much is lost by giving a wide berth to a few areas that could ruin your whole day.

Beach Driving Dangers

Regarding driving one's car on a Pacific coastal beach, it is well known that it is necessary to stay out of the water-swept portion of the beach on one side and the dry sand on the other. I am referring to the surf-pounded beaches as found from Baja through California, Oregon, Washington and British Columbia. For newcomers and tourists to these flat beaches where driving is allowed, the facts of life about beach driving are not well known, so there are unfortunate incidents. For the many rescues performed each year by regional beach patrols and local commercial tow trucks, there are still a number of automobiles lost to the incoming tides along the Oregon and Washington beaches.

Our son Dick and some friends on an Oregon beach trip came

across the desperate situation of a stuck camper and boat trailer. A wheat rancher from Montana who was unfamiliar with the beach sands had turned out toward the surf and was up to the axles with the incoming tide. From out of nowhere an elderly gentleman walked up to the group and said: "If you will do exactly as I say, we all can get you out of this. Now, first disconnect the boat trailer and run it up to the edge of the beach." Without any questions, the rancher, his wife, and the four young men did exactly that. Then he said, "The plan now is to unload the camper—everything," and they did that. "Now get on each side of the truck. We are going to lift the chassis straight up as much as we can, hold, then ease it down. Each time we do this, a little bit of sand will move in under the tires. It may take a dozen or more times. I will do the calling, 'one, two, three, lift, hold, one, two, three, down,' and we will rest between each cycle." They all did just as the old man directed, and he, too, did his share of the work. In a surprisingly short time the truck was raised enough to allow them to push it away from the rising tide. The boys helped to load up the camper and hook on the trailer. The rancher and his wife were trying to think of some way to show their gratitude for the assistance, when one of the boys said, "Where did that old man go to?" Sure enough, he was gone—the same way he had arrived.

Although you may not find yourself in the situation described above, there are a number of other cautions that will apply to you if you drive on Pacific beaches. When driving the beach at night, go at a moderate speed and be careful. One driver at night ran into a shipwrecked hull and put everyone in the hospital. Even in the daytime, watch out for the swales and small streams—they may have soft bottoms. My general rule for driving a beach is—*don't,* unless your car has large-sized low-pressure tires. Furthermore, recent regulations on beach driving in Oregon and Washington prohibit driving in some areas depending on the month and the time of day (See Chapter 4). I have never actually experienced any quicksand on Pacific coast beaches, but I have been on sand and mud flats that made walking nearly impossible.

Exposure and Other Human Dangers

Exposure is a hazard of the beachcomber. The effects of too

much sun and not enough covering are well known. The effects of hiking in damp clothing in a chilling snowstorm for miles along some beach can be serious. At lower temperatures, the wind chill factor is almost always present on the beach. However, if you keep your head warm and your feet dry, you can go for a full day in almost any weather on almost any beach. This assumes in the winter that you wear light raingear over wool clothing and that you take along food and fresh water.

If your beachcombing is thwarted by a fair sized stream or small river that is too deep to wade across, the alternatives are to swim or to build a raft. For either alternative, be sure you are prepared for the consequences before you proceed. It is one thing to be with a group in the summer and have all the necessary means to cross—rope to build a raft, nails, poles—but quite another situation to want to ferry a rain-swollen river in November by yourself with no makings of a raft nearby.

Suppose you slip from a rock or sandbar and are carried out to sea. From the standpoint of survival, what should be done? What should not be done? Perhaps here we can take a lesson from the offshore sailing yachtsmen. In conjunction with these yachtsmen, several doctors at the University of Victoria, British Columbia, have recently undertaken some immersion and survival research titled "Project Man Overboard." In their initial report, it is emphasized that the lowering of human body temperature rather than drowning is the basic cause of ocean water fatalities. It is important to protect the temperature of such vital organs as the heart. The prime factors affecting the temperature drop of an individual are: temperature of the water, insulation of the clothing, thickness of the layer of the body fat, amount of swimming or struggling, psychological state regarding panic, and such physiological responses as shivering. If the normal heat production keeps pace with heat loss, body temperature will be maintained; if not, body cooling begins.

The results of this research indicate the following cardinal recommendations for someone who has inadvertently been immersed in the sea: keep calm, keep your clothes on, and keep from expending any more energy than absolutely necessary, especially by doing needless swimming. The don'ts are almost the opposite: don't panic, don't remove what clothes you have on because they may help to hold in body heat, don't reduce your body energy heat source by swimming, especially if swimming won't be effective in reaching land.

There is a hazard of getting lost in the thick underbrush found along a Pacific Northwest coast beach when going inland to avoid an impossible headland or to take a shortcut. This is particularly likely during foggy weather — a time when the ocean surf is apt not to be heard for any great distance, and losing the sound of the surf is the easiest way to become disoriented. Managing a footing in the thick salal (a small shrub common along the Pacific coast) and other coastal growth can be a real chore. Many a time I have gone inland to find myself walking on thickly intertwined limbs and branches without ever setting foot on ground. Trying to find one's way through such a coastal jungle, while searching for a footing in the fog without a pocket compass, has a way of changing one's attitudes. The feeling of being lost in this thick growth is like being caught in the fog off Vancouver Island in a small boat.

When beachcombing, be especially alert to man-made dangers. Watch for fires left from the previous day or night by someone else. The wind-fanned wood coals travel long distances and even continue to burn underneath the sand. I have seen fires left over from the previous day by careless campers that have taken off and gone up a bank of dry brush for several hundred feet and over wide areas. Watch for the still hot metal pieces, straps, driftbolts, and fittings from timbers that were left in random fashion around a fire site.

As a final caution, do your long beachcombing treks buddy fashion, two by two, and keep in sight of one another. Some of the younger beachcombers want to do their combing hand in hand, but this practice will get a little tiring if done for the seven beach miles per day that I am talking about. Beachcombing, to be successful, is essentially a problem of range; to bring back the prizes, you have to cover many miles in the few days that are reserved for this fun activity. Ideally, two couples make the best beachcombing team for the average Pacific coastal beach, which is usually wide and flat with a lot of area to cover. Always start your beach hike up wind—this provides the tail wind on the way back when you need it the most.

Notwithstanding the dangers along the shores of the Pacific, the advantages of living adjacent to or by the sea are to be applauded. How delightful it is to be able to walk the same beach all year around. How rewarding it is after a lengthy overcast spell to enjoy a beautiful sunny windless day with the pounding surf. The principal dividend of living by the sea is regularly beachcombing a familiar beach, knowing when and where to look for all the things that wash ashore. A friend finds an occasional arrowhead at one ocean beach that she combs almost every day.

Beachcombers are provided the anticipation of the unexpected, the unknown, and the rare item along our shores of the great Pacific Ocean — despite its unforgivingness to those ignorant of her ways.

Cool Pacific feels good after beachcombing hot beach sands at Leadbetter Point, Washington, in August with Mount St. Helens sprewing steam ninety miles inland. (Author Photo)

Extensive beach drift on outer coast of Vancouver Island provides year round beachcombing. (Author Photo)

7
Major Expeditions

Before relating the highlights of similar but varied major beach-combing expeditions, it should be pointed out that some well-planned operations are carried out in simple terms of money, equipment, and time; while others are conducted in a more elaborate and extensive fashion. But, no matter how limited or extensive an expedition you plan, you will need to consider where to go, how many people to include, what equipment to take, and what preparation will be necessary—all topics discussed in this chapter.

For many people of modest means who are regularly tied to their work or family, a major beachcombing expedition would be, for example, to travel from the midwestern part of our country to the California coast. There they might walk the sandy shores of Marin County in California, finding shells and driftwood to bring home as evidence of a carefree Pacific Ocean beachcombing expedition. This might take about ten days of their vacation.

On the other end of the spectrum, for those more affluent of the jet set, a major beachcombing expedition might mean flying to a distant global spot having exotic surroundings. People of this lifestyle might fly to an isolated locale, then charter a small airplane to shuttle them to a small island that has, as its first requirement, lodgings that would provide all the necessary creature comforts for the month's stay.

In between these two groups are an expanding number of Americans who take their vacations via commercial jet to some resort that may be at the other end of the country, and more than likely includes a beach area.

Where to Go

There are many fine beaches around the Pacific Ocean that could be visited on an expedition; many are on our own continent along California, Oregon, and Washington shores. However, an expedition to the Caroline Islands or Marshall Islands in the far Pacific might stretch the budget of a retired schoolteacher from Des Moines, Iowa. If Baja were selected, it would be necessary to purchase considerable equipment to make that all-terrain-vehicle trek across the Vizcaino desert, much more than one might choose to buy for a two-week period. If the Aleutians are to be sought out, plan on considerable air travel, much by bush pilot, with a final drop at a location where food and shelter will consist of what you carry in your backpack—and bring a rifle for protection. Hawaii is fine, but all those new hotels contain people like you who went there, among other reasons, to walk the beaches. The Queen Charlotte Islands in British Columbia are isolated enough, but many beaches are only available by boat.

Such a journey or expedition need not be to a faraway land or involve elaborate logistics to achieve the specific purposes. Indeed, a major expedition might be many things to many people. It might mean no more than the drive from Sacramento, California, to Point Arena on the coast—a distance of 160 miles—in order to spend the day looking for pieces of oriental beach woods. In any case, whether the expedition destination is faraway or near at hand, the anticipation, planning, and preparation for a beachcombing trip to an isolated location in another state or country would be equally as exciting as the actual event regardless of what location you might select.

How Many to Include

How many people should be included in an expedition? It could range from one to a dozen. Certainly, the greatest mobility is gained when you go by yourself because the response to objectives and changes in travel plans will be immediate. I know of a trout fisherman who travels worldwide by himself with complete ease and freedom. Likewise, a solo backpacking beachcombing expedition to southern Alaska in the summertime would be most enjoyable.

Two people have considerable mobility, and if they are socially compatible they will readily fit the patterns associated with travel and lodging. During the beachcombing, two people can operate conveniently as a team in which each covers a separate strip of the beach.

Four people, or two couples, usually make for a comfortable sized group, particularly if they have known one another before undertaking the expedition. With four people, however, the mobility lessens considerably because the total can move only as fast as the slowest person.

A six-person group is fine for a major beach hike whatever the mix may be with regard to couples. Such a group at the beach may revert to any combination of singles and couples depending on immediate interests. When the group is to break up into opposite directions for tide line searching, it will often break up into two groups of three, each group going their separate way.

With eight people, the group approaches the maximum size unless they are four dedicated couples experienced at beach hiking, in which case they will operate as four individual teams. I think ten people are about the upper limit for working an ocean beach since its natural confines make it essentially linear in dimension. Incidentally, once such a party starts down a beach, any leadership disappears as the individuals soon get out of earshot—a serious concern when youngsters are included in the group. Groups of one, two, or three will stretch out depending on the experience of the individuals. A person new to the beach will walk at a good pace on the hard sand at the high tide line in order to reach the far end of the beach. An experienced beachcomber will mosey along in a zigzag manner, stepping from log to log along the top of the drift. Ten people will string out over a long distance in a short period of time; however, after the day's walk, members of such a large group will start getting in each other's way when crammed into the cabin, or hopefully cabins. In these circumstances, a three-day outing is about the limit of human tolerance and endurance.

Equipment

The equipment required for a beachcombing expedition can be as simple as a paper sack to carry shells or as elaborate as a four-truck operation supplemented with an airplane and a helicopter. I like to think that an expedition should not be a show of the financial level of resources available to an individual; otherwise, it has the taint of a salvage operation.

In general, each person who is a part of a group perusing a beach should be garbed for the elements and should carry as much gear as is required to perform the task he chooses to accomplish. For example, one friend of mine on an expedition only wanted to search for agates, so he brought portable sifting trays and a short-handled shovel in his backpack. For him, the agates he hoped to dig out of the gravel were going to be worth the labor of carrying the trays and shovel five miles down the beach and five miles back.

I find that a small hand saw is useful in cutting samples of woods from larger planks or limbs, yet I would not recommend a hand saw in a list of equipment for the average beachcomber unless he is interested in oriental woods. In other words, equipment, like the choice of a site and the number of expedition members, is largely a matter of personal needs and desires.

Preparation

The planning and preparation for a beachcombing expedition is the first half of the total adventure. Selecting and deciding on the objectives sets the expedition in motion. One can even afford the luxury of daydreaming about the intended goals of the expedition. Then comes the implementation of each step of the adventure. Charts of the beach areas to be assaulted are fully as important as land maps and should be acquired. Charts show all sorts of information—where the flat sandy areas begin, where the headlands must be climbed at high tide, and where there are marshy river entrances. Clothing and equipment lists need to be started, and added to. The full gamut of possible weather conditions should be considered.

Read all that is available in order to find out about the area. When possible, interview people who have been there. There is no substitute for doing one's homework before starting off. Without proper preparation, the best intended expedition can be a continual series of disappointments, so plan ahead. The anticipation of success of a well-prepared expedition can be so powerful that the actual discovery of what you had set out to do will seem anticlimactic.

A Family Beachcombing Expedition

We have made a number of highly successful two-family vacation beachcombing trips in summertime to British Columbia and Alaskan coastal areas. These consisted of two families that had known one another for several years. The original matching of the families should contain facets of common interest because the rigors of camping out soon will test all of the individuals included. Our operating plan called for two cars, two tents, and two small boats. We fished inland lakes en route and did everything buddy system. We also invited along a friend or two of the youngsters to be sure each person had a vacation partner for the fishing and beachcombing.

During these two-week family expeditions, we traveled, fished, camped, and beachcombed in about equal proportions. For the beachcombing, we held contests with prizes given out at a dinner party after we returned home. The prizes were for different categories —the most artistic item found, the most practical, the most valuable, the least valuable, and the most unusual.

Regarding equipment for such an expedition, each family took a tent, sleeping bags, air mattresses, cooking utensils, dishpans, camping seats, lantern, ax, insect spray, and food. Personal clothing and effects for each person meant separate luggage, including waterproof gear, jackets, and boots. A folding table and cooking stove were considered communal items. With each boat, we took an outboard engine, oars, life preservers, fishing equipment, and ice chest.

To prepare for these beachcombing expeditions, several joint planning sessions were held. First we decided on the objectives and the route. Then we selected the menu. Study of the maps provided us with the choice of likely campsites along the way and at the ocean. We planned to reach these campsites by early afternoon in order to avoid having to pitch the tents at night in heavy rains, a circumstance that always seemed to be a disaster when it did happen.

We carried dehydrated foods plus other items that wouldn't take much volume. Fresh water was never a problem in the wilds of British Columbia with all the freshwater lakes there. In all, about forty meals had to be planned. We depended on rice, buckwheat flour, and spaghetti to carry the theme of the meal planning around the fish we expected to catch and the berries we planned to pick. We would go through small towns en route and fishing villages at the ocean, so an occasional purchase of fresh vegetables, fruit, and meat would supplement the larder.

Planning also meant seeing that all the equipment was operating properly. Stove, lantern, air mattresses, outboard and fishing equipment all needed to be tested to insure that they were fully functional. A prepared list of things to bring, which was cross-checked with the other family, was most useful. Special equipment required for beachcombing was aimed principally at clothing and footgear that would resist driving wind and rain.

Family beachcombing trips such as this, particularly when they are recorded on film and in a notebook, provide a wealth of memories for each member of the expedition. Years later, the conversation may include, "I will never forget that time with the Closes when we had to leave the Indian dugout canoe behind . . ." or, "Remember when we were at Ketchikan with the Davises. . . ." Having been there, it is hard to block out the roar of the surf, the cry of the gulls, and the family fun of going barefoot in the sand while searching the tide lines.

A Special Beachcombing Expedition

Suppose, for the purpose of illustration, that you receive the following invitation: "You are cordially invited to our annual beachcomber get-together the third week in March at Tofino, British Columbia. RSVP by February 15 for reservations." "Where is Tofino, and why in March?" you would ask.

As the head of the planning committee, allow me to answer. At a relatively isolated coastal area on the outer western shore of Vancouver Island is a small end-of-the-road fishing village. It is located near prime beachcombing areas that front the Pacific Ocean's North Pacific Current. After traveling from the Orient for about one thousand days, flotsam contained within this current is carried to our western American continent at this latitude. March is the best month because of ocean storms that drive floating debris shoreward.

After responding to the invitation, you would receive travel instructions that would read essentially as follows: "Take nonstop flight to Seattle, transfer to Air Canada for Vancouver, British Columbia. Here there are two options. The first, weather permitting, is to fly West Coast Air Services directly to Tofino. The alternative is to rent a car, take oceangoing B. C. Ferry System to Nanaimo on Vancouver Island, and drive the fifty miles to Port Alberni. Here prepare for 85 miles of winter driving across the island without benefit of gas station, house, store, or sign of habitation. This means preparation for possible emergencies along the way such as snowslides, trees that have fallen across the road, and flooding. An ax, shovel, blankets, and food are recommended, along with a full tank of gas. Snowslides might cut off travel for several days."

Needless to say, the first option of flying in is to be preferred over the alternative of driving; however, bad weather is what provides good beachcombing. Once at Tofino, whether you arrived at the airport or at the village center, you would be met in order to transfer you and your baggage by small boat to Stubbs Island where Clayoquot Inn sprawls in placid fashion, our rendezvous and lodging for the following week.

The suggested clothing list would run: thermal underwear, woolen sweaters and pants, waterproofs or full-length parkas, rain-resistant shoes or knee-length fisherman's boots, and rain headgear. The beachcombing equipment list would include rucksack, trowel, sunglasses, gloves, and rain tarp for temporary shelter. Appropriate lodge wear and final dinner party clothes would also be included.

Daily beachcombing trips would be made by small boat, weather permitting, to islands further north such as Vargas, Flores, Bartlett, and Blunden—all of which have both exposed and protected beaches. Breakfast and dinner would be at the Inn, and food baskets for lunch would be taken in each boat. A daily beachcombing task would be established, such as looking for driftwood that resembled animals or shell collections. Should the weather make travel impossible to the other islands, then substitute tasks for hikes would be arranged. Clams could be dug or oysters might be harvested.

The schedule for the week might be:

Sunday	Travel to Tofino
Monday	Vargas Island trip
Tuesday	Blunden Island trip
Wednesday	Flores Island trip
Thursday	Bartlett Island trip
Friday	Free day and final dinner party
Saturday	Travel to Vancouver, B. C., and home

Our group would consist of eight people, preselected for the occasion by virtue of special abilities or avocations. Each member would be given and be aware of a special function, such as the expedition poet, artist, photographer, movie photographer, music writer, author, or philosopher. Alternate capabilities such as a botanist, meteorologist, historian, zoologist, and geologist might be substituted. Before the expedition, it would be made clear that one of the requirements of each job would be to share individual findings and observations about the expedition at the Friday evening dinner party. Any original work done during the expedition would not be divulged until the dinner party. Perhaps a limit of fifteen minutes per performance would be advisable.

The after-dinner program would consist first of awarding prizes for the daily tasks and overall established categories. Second, from this group of people:

- the poet would read poetry composed during the expedition
- the photographer would tell of the images captured on film
- the artist would show and critique original works conceived during the expedition
- the movie photographer would explain whatever film had come out of the week's activities
- the music writer would play original music composed during the week
- the author would read original musings and observations
- the philosopher would present ideas appropriate to the occasion

• the host would collect the writings and photographs for the preparation of a booklet to record the adventure

Thus, the culmination of this expedition would be the capturing of the innovations of an unstructured, creative, free-wheeling group in a situation in which personal contributions would be shared.

This expedition would have the benefits of lodge amenities yet would be located at the very edge of isolation. We would see eagles and marine mammals. While boating to the islands, we would wave at the Indians in their dugouts from the nearby Clayoquot Indian Reservation at Opitsat. We would feel the fury of the Pacific as it smashes against the rocky shores.

The daily voyage to the designated beachcombing tasks would mean about an hour run each way by boat. Each beach would be loaded with driftwood, far more than could be properly combed that day. While one boatload of four people would be at one island, the second boat would be at another. Both boats would return to the Clayoquot Inn in late afternoon in time for tea by the fireplace, followed by a nap and dinner.

After-dinner entertainment would consist of short talks by Tofino residents on the geography, history, flora and fauna, and Indian culture of the region. Every night you would sleep soundly under two blankets.

Back home, after this eventful week, the shells, floats, driftwood, and other oriental evidence would grace your mantlepiece to remind you of the vast Pacific and of one group effort that sought to understand it all.

I can assure you that this suggested expedition is quite real—I have participated in just such an expedition. All it takes to make it come true for you as well is the will to do something beyond the humdrum pattern of your daily doings.

8
Armchair Beachcombing

When the snow is flying outside, I take a lot of beachcombing trips to the far corners of the Pacific Ocean without ever leaving the comfort of my Mercer Island living room. All that is required is a hankering to seek an undiscovered place on a chart.

Navigation charts are rolled open on the living room floor rug. These show all the coastal characteristics of the region. I also gather maps of my selected region, get background information from the library, and spread all this out in front of the fireplace on a winter Sunday evening.

Instantly I fly my living room magic carpet to a mysterious beach off the northern side of the Aleutians or to the northwestern corner of Vancouver Island. There I hike one area, then another, giving no thought to the problem of getting across the headland in between. About the time I am fording the river emptying into a bay shown on the chart, Elaine wakes me out of my fanciful travel with a tray of home-canned Vancouver Island salmon, crackers, cheese, and tea. We munch and chat. I do some more exploring, then fly home again.

I have actually explored many beaches that I had armchair beachcombed the winter before. At Kutcous Point, British Columbia,

Elaine and I found the rocks a bit sporty, but the river was easy to cross thanks to some logs we lashed together. The confirmation of walking a beach, earlier discovered on the chart by a warm fire, gives a great feeling of accomplishment and is worth all the involved and troublesome transportation logistics.

There is a small island I want to visit that is about 25 miles west of Cape Scott on Vancouver Island. This speck on the chart named Triangle Island is situated close to the Kuroshio Current. The island's beaches might provide samples of what the current is carrying this season. Over 300 yellow plastic buoys containing self-winding wrist-watches made by the Citizen Watch Company, Limited, of Tokyo were thrown into the Pacific off northern Japan as a research project —maybe one is waiting to be found on Triangle Island (only two from an earlier test have been reported found).

Armchair beachcombing does not end here. We take a lot of photographs; every time these are shown to friends, it means that they too can fly with us to a distant area to leave their footprints in the sand on these same beaches that I discovered on some charts spread out on the living room floor.

During these armchair cruises there is always the speculation about the probable course of events involving some of the more mysterious disappearances that have occurred in the past. Many a sailing ship has left a Pacific port never to be heard from again.

Yachts, kayaks, ships, and airplanes still challenge the Pacific, and not a few of these challenges have met with unwitnessed endings. Some of these happenings undoubtedly leave telltale debris to drift on the ocean in natural courses, directed by the major ocean currents. When the debris is blown ashore to come to rest along the beaches, clues may be available to help unravel these mysterious disappearances. The following tales are but a few of the more famous disappearances, but perhaps they will serve to fuel your imagination.

Amelia Earhart

As was widely reported by the press at the time, world-famous Amelia Earhart and navigator Fred Noonan were lost somewhere in the Pacific Ocean during a round-the-world flight in July 1937. Taking off from Lae, New Guinea, they failed to arrive at Howland

Island, their destination on that leg of their flight. Radio signals died at about the time the fuel supply ran out, so it was presumed they had missed their destination, a tiny mid-Pacific island.

I well remember Amelia Earhart and this flying laboratory airplane. She was then on the staff at Purdue University while I was a student there. Her shiny new twin-engine Lockheed Electra was kept in the Purdue University airport hangar alongside our secondary glider that we flew daily, teaching fledglings the techniques of gliding and soaring. Shortly before her last flight I had occasion to inspect the airplane, noting that the seats had been removed to make way for auxiliary fuel tanks and other equipment.

When she was reported overdue, it was assumed that the airplane had ditched in the sea and that they would be rescued. However, because of bad weather and high seas, the airplane presumably sank. Since then, having spent some time as an aircraft accident investigator, I learned that many times airplane parts will float for long periods of time to leave telltale evidence of a crash at sea.

Since Howland Island is directly in the path of the westbound South Equatorial Current that moves along at the high rate of 36 miles per day, I have since surmised that wreckage pieces could have headed west toward Guam or the Philippines, and then worked north to catch the powerful Kuroshio heading past Japan.

At the time of her disappearance, this strong current pattern may have been overlooked in the search that was conducted. In any event, such pieces could have floated from the Howland Island area in ocean currents to touch on American shores in about 2,100 days. This would date the arrival on the West Coast about the summer of 1943; however, it is possible that the debris continued to drift in the North Pacific circuit without getting beached anywhere.

In the summer of 1943, my estimated time for the arrival of this debris, I was beachcombing the Pacific Ocean inland waters of Puget Sound and the Straits of Juan de Fuca in the Pacific Northwest. These straits look directly out at the Pacific with its Kuroshio Current. If any pieces of airplane NR16020 had washed up at these locations where I was beachcombing, I could have identified them. Based on many of the things that came from other places in the Pacific Ocean that were beachcombed at that time, it is conceivable that I would have found parts of NR16020.

To the best of my knowledge, no part of her airplane was ever beachcombed. However, I would still like to think that high on a jack-straw pile of drift logs in an isolated area of the Queen Charlotte Islands is a piece of the landing gear or a portion of the tail from that historic airplane, perched up there waiting for someone to discover it.

Author Fred Goerner, in his book *The Search for Amelia Earhart*, gives a different note to any hopes of finding pieces of her airplane in the Queen Charlotte Islands. He proposes that at about 10:30 A.M. on the morning of July 2, 1937, Amelia Earhart and Fred Noonan made an emergency wheels up landing at Mili Atoll in the southeastern portion of the Marshall Islands and became prisoners of the Japanese. He believes they were involved in a 1937 version of a U-2 reconnaissance mission. He believes that the Japanese transported her airplane back to headquarters in Saipan, but that some seven years later, after United States forces had captured Saipan, this airplane was rolled out of a closely guarded hangar and destroyed.

If there were a water crash landing, as I believe there was, any beachcombed debris from airplane NR16020 would confirm that belief. If one accepts Goerner's sequence of probable events, no debris would have been set free to be picked up by the currents of the northern Pacific Ocean.

What really happened to Amelia Earhart is still a mystery; however, Goerner has presented an exceedingly convincing case. Others also have presented their theories. As a beachcomber, I would like to push Goerner's thesis to one side, but as an engineer, I find the evidence he has presented difficult to refute. As I walk the Pacific Ocean beaches, I think about his explanation but, nevertheless, continue to kick at the bark at the high tide line in hopes of finding a piece of this airplane.

Richard Halliburton

On a dark March night in 1939 during a wild mid-Pacific storm, a Chinese junk named the *Sea Dragon* vanished, presumably carrying its crew, including world-famous adventurer and author Richard Halliburton, to a watery grave. The junk was about one-third of the way across the Pacific on a 7,000-mile trip from Hong Kong to San Francisco when radio contact was lost. Typhoon weather with 40-

mile-per-hour winds and 40-foot seas was also reported by passenger ships in the same area. The last radio message from the *Sea Dragon* stated that they were encountering a southerly gale in a heavy rain squall on a true course of 100 degrees and at a position of 31 degrees north and 155 degrees east. This location put the junk at about 150 miles east of a small island named Ganges and about 1,600 miles west of Midway Island. The course direction indicated that the *Sea Dragon* was heading for the Hawaiian Islands rather than directly for San Francisco.

It is believed that during the gale and heavy seas the *Sea Dragon* lost her rudder, broached, foundered, and sank. Similar rudder problems had plagued junk designs as far back as 1639. Stability and control characteristics for junks of that early day were a matter of imperial edict, not high seas requirements.

Floating debris believed to have been from the *Sea Dragon* was sighted sixteen months later about 1,200 miles east of the last-known position. Unfortunately this debris was not picked up for identification. However, my study of ocean surface currents at that location indicates that the released debris probably headed a different direction. The last-known position of the *Sea Dragon* was too far south to have been caught in the strong eastbound Kuroshio Current; instead it followed the local drift, which was toward the southeast, and then turned westward toward China. In the vicinity of Okinawa such debris could have caught the northbound Kuroshio and then headed east toward western American shores. This drift voyage would take roughly 1,700 days, making its estimated time of arrival no sooner than January 1944. At that time, since much of our western coast was under military control, little beachcombing by civilian residents who formerly patrolled the shores on a regular basis was allowed. Oddly enough, a portion of a wooden keel with ribs attached, thought by some to be from the *Sea Dragon* was beachcombed at Pacific Beach, California, in 1945—only 450 miles south of San Francisco, Halliburton's destination. However, no verification ever took place due to overriding wartime concerns. Thus, the date of the earliest possible arrival of any wreckage on our western shores via the Kuroshio Current is very close to assumed current routes and speeds.

Had any debris kept going instead of beaching that year, the currents in the northern Pacific would have carried it for another nine years before getting back to this side again, assuming the wood planking had not become water soaked by then. Gooseneck barnacles, which attach themselves to planks and bottles, will cause the weight to go up and sink such items below the surface.

When the *Sea Dragon* broke up, the engine and ballast certainly took the main hull to the bottom some three miles below. When it hit, it must have broken off more pieces. Parts would break away and pop up to the surface for some time, thus the floating debris would be strung out for a long distance.

Is there any possibility of beachcombing parts of the *Sea Dragon* today? Yes, I think there is, assuming that the original woods were identified. Perhaps a study could be made of the woods that were used in ship construction at Hong Kong shipyards in 1939. There may be such pieces of wood on the British Columbia coast at such locations as Cox Bay, a place I would like to think I know as well as the back of my hand.

Perhaps those who have read Halliburton's books and have been touched by the Halliburton myth may want to believe that he is still alive somewhere. As a professional beachcomber, I believe that pieces of the *Sea Dragon* could be resting this very moment at isolated beaches in Alaska or Baja, Mexico. All it takes is for another adventurer with a bent similar to that of Richard Halliburton's to start looking. Samples of oriental woods will have to be obtained, the age determined, and results communicated with others.

For those who live on the threshold of the world's finest beachcombing, why not also look for the gold and scarlet painted *Sea Dragon?* What happened to Richard Halliburton? Did he really land on some Pacific island only to be killed by the natives?

The Tonquin

Perhaps one of the most baffling yet dramatic episodes of early Pacific Northwest history concerns the fur trading ship *Tonquin* that John Jacob Astor sent to the Columbia River in 1810. Capitalizing on reports from Lewis and Clark of plentiful fur-bearing animals throughout this territory, Astor fitted out two expeditions to establish a fur trading post at the mouth of the Columbia River. This strategic position in the fur trade was of such importance that Astor sent one expedition by land and the other by sea to be sure of success.

When his British competitors heard of this, they also outfitted a land expedition, which made it an international race. The Astor sea party arrived first, thanks to the determination of its ship captain Jonathan Thorn and some fifty crew and passengers, all aboard the *Tonquin*. Because a fur trading post and fort was established at Astoria, Oregon, by the Astor party in 1811, later American claims to this territory were upheld after the British had taken the fort away from the Astor organization. Thus, we residents of Oregon and Washington today speak with an Illinois or Minnesota accent, rather than in a British accent as do our neighbors in British Columbia.

The *Tonquin* was prepared for departure from Astoria soon after arrival, for a three-month fur trading voyage northward to Sitka and back. Astor had a cargo of gunpowder consigned to the Russian Commissar Baranof. On June 5, 1811, the *Tonquin* sailed away from the Columbia River never to be seen again by any white man. Presumably its first stop was Vancouver Island to trade with the Nootkan tribes. In a short time, the native's moccasin telegraph told the Indians back at the Columbia River that the ship had met with disaster at the hands of Vancouver Island Indians. Much later, an Indian interpreter came to Astoria and claimed he was present to witness the capture of the ship by the Wickaninnish tribe, and on the following day, an unexplained explosion that blew the ship and a number of Indians aboard her at the time clear to kingdom come. The ship sank, and to this day, no one knows for sure where the ship remains rest. There were no white witnesses, no white survivors, no on-the-spot press coverage.

There have been numerous expeditions to the waters of Clayoquot Sound on Vancouver Island to try to locate the ship's remains, but all have failed. I undertook two expeditions of my own in recent years but have yet to uncover any positive findings. I did uncover a wealth of Indian history about this event, enough to convince me that it did happen within the general territory of the Clayoquot tribe.

There was no gold aboard this ship to attract treasure seekers, only anchors and cannon to tease the historical artifact collector. Yet to mention the name *Tonquin* is enough to pour adrenalin into the veins of the most casual of West Coast beachcombers, for it is generally agreed that the explosion of nine tons of gunpowder sent plenty of pieces of the Tonquin in numerous directions to lodge in the sands of nearby beaches. If you want to learn of this beautiful sailing ship and its dramatic demise, read the account of this incident in Washington Irving's *Astoria*; I assure you that you will never be the same again.

Spanish Galleon

Since we tend to think of Spanish galleon traffic taking place in the Atlantic Ocean, Caribbean Sea, or nearby equatorial waters, it is a surprise to many people to learn that Spanish galleons plied the northern Pacific and could have come as far north as Oregon. That the highly profitable Spanish Manila galleon operations could have lost one or more of its vessels on the Oregon coast is not only possible but also quite likely, thanks to the Kuroshio Current.

Coastal Indian oral history, writings of early explorers and fur traders, plus the findings of beachcombers confirm the probable shipwreck of a Spanish galleon, possibly two, in the vicinity of the Oregon coast between Nehalem Spit and the Columbia River. Study of eastbound routes taken by Spanish Manila galleon pilots from Manila to Acapulco shows that a storm-wrecked galleon, rudderless and demasted, might easily have drifted in Pacific Ocean currents to come to its final resting place in the surf of an Oregon beach.

Considerable has been written about the Indian legends and explorers' reports regarding the existence of a Spanish galleon shipwreck; thus, for our interest, I will stick to actual beachcombing findings of ships' parts and cargo. Although wreckage from two ships was sighted on the Oregon coast as early as 1844, and as late as 1898, no specific locations were recorded and no samples of woods and metal parts were preserved from these wrecks. The sightings, locations, and findings seem to have been lost in the intervening years.

What happens when a ship comes too close to a sandy beach of the Pacific Ocean? It is caught in the surf and driven into the beach. In a short time, the powerful wave action tears the structure apart and buries it in the sand to slowly disappear from view. Seasonal changes in the sand level on the beach may expose the ship rib carriage for a short while, but in a few months' time, it is covered over again.

After a period of time, only short stubs of ribs get uncovered by the shifting beach sands.

Some wreckage is driven up at high tide into the sandbanks that occur all along the ocean front, to be covered and then uncovered for a short time. The natural cycle of the sandbank sloughing away and the high tides washing away the banks will cover and uncover as mentioned; however, few wrecks have been driven that far up to escape the clutches and hammering action of the surf.

Unfortunately it is not possible to point to even a single barnacle-covered stub sticking out of the flat sand that would confirm the reports of a Spanish galleon wreck. A possible way of confirming the occurrence of such a wreck would be to track down some canes and walking sticks reportedly fashioned by a beachcomber in 1898 from teak timbers taken from a ship's wreckage near Manzanita, Oregon.

Another approach to solving this mystery is for some dedicated beachcomber to start a project of looking for old ship timbers between Nehalem Spit and the Columbia River. He would first have to find out what types of wood were used in ship construction in Manila from 1565 to 1815. Then he would have to obtain samples of these same woods for comparison purposes. Finally, each and every likely-looking timber sticking out from a sandbank, as well as every plank beyond the line of vegetation, would have to be checked to see if it matched the grain of the samples. This might show that there was a high incidence of teakwood in a quarter-mile location. If that were so, the possible location of a wreck out in the surf could be determined.

So, the evidence of a shipwreck that was so clear to all at one time is, for all practical purposes, lost. The legends and stories of treasure being brought ashore and buried on Neahkahnie Mountain go on, but the pinpointing of a wreck is still the secret of the sea. Here is a challenge of major proportion for present and future hikers of the Pacific Ocean Oregon seashore.

. . . pleasant summer hours . . . (Author Photo)

. . . pleasant winter hours . . . (Author Photo)

Postscript

We have spent many pleasant hours walking Pacific Ocean beaches, admiring the continuous assault of its waves onto flat broad expanses and watching at its very edge the release of the energy that has been pent up for thousands of miles. Where ocean waves attack a rocky coast, we keep our distance to watch the conflict as a spectator. It is back on the flat sandy shores that our wanderings bring us inner peace. The dividends of a small shell, a few pieces of driftwood, and whatever other souvenirs that we may pocket for later display subtly suggest further non-essential conquests.

At home, I have a room I call my beachcomber study. Mounted on the walls are our beachcombed trophies. Not everything we find is considered a trophy, only those outstanding items that another beachcomber would admire. The mere presence of these trophies brings to mind many successful expeditions. The red Japanese fishing fleet flag, the wristwatch buoy, the Nootkan Chief Maquinna hat, the ivory whale tooth, the argillite Haida carving, the piece of Manila galleon beeswax, the slices of exotic wood, the sailing ship deadeye, the agates, and the glass floats—all tell of our beachcombing exploits around the North Pacific Rim.

My beachcomber study is also haven for dozens of rolled up

charts depicting beach areas from Alaska to Guam, as well as maps of nearby land areas. On one wall are framed photographs, an original oil painting by Manning de V. Lee, an Anton Roux ship print, two ship models, and a Samurai sword. Our glass float collection is elsewhere, out in the family room.

Were it ever necessary to dispose of these blue-green oriental spheres, rather than see them fall out of favor and be sent to the Salvation Army, we have a fail-safe plan. We will package them in boxes, give the entire lot to some Orient-bound tramp steamer captain with instructions to drop them piece by piece on his way west across the vast Pacific Ocean. In this way, another generation of beachcombers will find and admire these as we have done.

. . . another generation . . . (Author Photo)

Bibliography

Bascom, Willard. *Waves and Beaches: The Dynamics of the Ocean Surface*. New York: Doubleday, 1964.

Berg, Norah. *Lady on the Beach*. Englewood Cliffs, New Jersey: Prentice-Hall, 1952.

Carey, Neil G. *Puffin Cove*. Blaine, Wash.: Hancock House, 1982.

Franchere, Gabriel. *Adventure at Astoria, 1810-1814*. Norman, Oklahoma: University of Oklahoma Press, 1967.

Gibbons, Euell. *Beachcombers Handbook*. New York: David McKay, 1967.

Goerner, Fred. *The Search for Amelia Earhart*. New York: Doubleday, 1966.

Hult, Ruby El. *Lost Mines and Treasures of the Pacific Northwest*. Portland, Oregon: Binfords & Mort, 1964.

Irving, Washington. *Astoria, or Anecdotes of an Enterprise Beyond the Rocky Mountains*. Norman, Oklahoma: University of Oklahoma Press, 1964.

McMahan, Mike. *There It Is: Baja*. Riverside, California: Manessier, 1973.

Root, Jonathan. *Halliburton the Magnificent Myth*. New York: Coward, McCann and Geoghegan, 1965.

Rudloe, Jack. *The Erotic Ocean: A Handbook for Beachcombers*. New York: World, 1972.

Schurz, William Lytle. *The Manila Galleon*. New York: E. P. Dutton, 1939.

Sharcott, Margaret. *Trollers Holiday*. Toronto: British Book Service, 1957.

Thompson, Bob. *Beachcombers Guide to the Pacific Coast*. Menlo Park, California: Lane, 1966.

Webber, Bert. *Beachcombing for Driftwood, for Glass Floats, for Agates, for Fun*. Fairfield, Washington: Ye Galleon Press, 1973.

———. *Retaliation: Japanese Attacks and Allied Countermeasures on the Pacific Coast in World War II*. Corvallis, Oregon: Oregon State University Press, 1975.

———. *What Happened at Bayocean—Is Salishan Next?* Fairfield, Washington: Ye Galleon Press, 1973.

Oregon: Binfords & Mort, 1971.

Wood, Amos L. *Beachcombing for Japanese Glass Floats.* Portland, Oregon: Binfords & Mort, fourth edition 1985.

_____ *Hiking Trails in the Pacific Northwest.* Matteson, Illinois: Greatlakes Living Press, 1977.

_____ *Best Hiking Trails in the United States.* Matteson, Illinois: Greatlakes Living Press, 1977.

Index

5198